SUPPER
CLUB

SUPPER CLUB

CREATIVE IDEAS FOR SMALL-GROUP FELLOWSHIP

EDITED BY

MICHAEL KENDRICK

Foreword by Carl F. George

Baker Books

A Division of Baker Book House Co
Grand Rapids, Michigan 49516

Published by Baker Books
a division of Baker Book House Company
P.O. Box 6287, Grand Rapids, Michigan 49516-6287

Printed in the United States of America

Library of Congress Cataloging-in-Publication Data

Kendrick, Michael, 1960–
    Supper club : creative ideas for small-group fellowship / edited by Michael Kendrick ;
    foreword by Carl F. George.
        p.   cm.
      ISBN 0-8010-5263-7
1. Church dinners. 2. Church group work. 3. Small groups.
I. Title.
BV1635.K46   1994
253'.7--dc20   94-17400

Produced by The Livingstone Corporation for Baker Book House. Michael Kendrick, David Veerman, and James C. Galvin, project staff.

CONTENTS

• • • • • • • •

FOREWORD

● ● ● ● ● ● ● ●

Supper Club provides a practical, creative, and entertaining set of tools for winning the hearts of newcomers to a church as well as for drawing in those who stand on the periphery of a church. These exercises, if combined with the strategic placement of group leaders and apprentice group leaders, will do more to welcome people hungry for community than scores of sermons could accomplish.

Every acquaintance-making opportunity in a church opens the door to the fellowship of that church. *Supper Club's* ready-made dinner-and-discussion format is a great asset for anyone who would speed that process.

Those churches familiar with meta-church theory will understand how important it is for a church to provide constant and intentional opportunities for people to get to know one another, because affinity is discovered in acquaintance. The creation of numerous acquaintance-making places encourages the networking needed between group leaders and prospects. As a result, the group life of a church is able to attract a higher percentage of would-be entrants to eventual membership.

May *Supper Club* offer a new "mezzanine floor" in your church, where people move from the anonymous to the known, and from the unacquainted to the welcomed.

Carl F. George

ACKNOWLEDGMENTS

• • • • • • • •

We would like to thank the following people for their marvelously creative ideas that made this book fun to write and assemble. The contributors are listed next to the particular evening plan(s) for which they submitted ideas.

Tim and Patty Atkins ....Walt Disney Evening
Tacky Evening
Star Trek Evening
Lifestyles of the Rich and
Famous Evening
TV Trivia Evening

Karen Ball ....Medieval Quest Evening

Linda Taylor ....1950s Evening
High School Reunion Evening

Len Woods ....1970s Evening

Neil Wilson ....International Evening
First-Century Church Evening

Jeff Wyatt .... All about Me Evening

A special thanks to Ann Fackler and Renée Richter for providing recipes.

If you have ideas for a supper club evening that others might enjoy, we'd like to hear about them. Please write to Michael Kendrick, The Livingstone Corporation, 351 Executive Drive, Carol Stream, IL 60188.

INTRODUCTION

• • • • • • • •

Small groups are becoming an increasingly important part of the life of a church. Over the past decade, the number of churches that have begun or expanded small-group fellowship groups has grown dramatically. Small groups have become popular for several reasons. First, they allow men and women the opportunity to develop deep-rooted friendships with other members of their church. Second, the small group provides a nonthreatening atmosphere for drawing visitors, seekers, and new members into the life of the church. Third, the small group often becomes a vital link for keeping church members aware of the needs and concerns of their congregation. For many, small groups have been a rescue from the impersonal circumstances of modern life.

All small groups must begin somewhere. That is why we have written *Supper Club: Creative Ideas for Small-Group Fellowship*. The supper club is a terrific idea for church members who want to start a small group with a memorable event. It is also a creative way to add variety to existing small groups or to welcome a new couple or person who may be looking to make new friendships.

The supper club idea has been used with great success by hundreds of churches across the nation. If you have ever participated in a dinner for six or eight, you know how fun and relaxing the evening can be. But if you've ever had to *host* such an event, you know how imposing the task can be. You probably asked yourself: What should I prepare? How do I keep the conversation from dragging? What kind of entertainment should I provide? How can I make that new person feel comfortable? Now there is a resource available to help you.

The emphasis in *Supper Club* is on creativity. We have organized the book around themes to make the evening easier to plan and more enjoyable for the guests. Some of the ideas may seem outlandish, but part of the reason for the craziness is that it allows people to open up and be themselves. Feel free to adapt the suggestions to suit your group.

To allay any fears, we have tried to anticipate some of the most common questions a potential host might ask.

Q. *How many people should I invite to the dinner?*
A. The evenings are designed for eight people, including the host(s). Groups of six to ten people, however, should be fine. Generally speaking, it's a good idea to include a mix of friends and new acquaintances. We have written *Supper Club* to work for all groups, single or married.

Q. *Should I invite unchurched people?*
A. In most cases, you can feel comfortable about inviting unchurched people. Obviously, some evenings will work better than others. The First-Century Church Evening, because it focuses extensively on Christian fellowship, may make an unchurched person uneasy. Most of the other evenings will work, though. You may need to adapt some of the discussion questions to fit your particular situation.

Q. *What should I keep in mind when choosing a theme for the evening?*
A. Think about the age and gender of your guests, as well as any common experiences that your group will have shared. Hosting a 1950s evening may not work well with a very young group. An older group might not get into the Disney theme. A group with more women than men may not enjoy the sports evening.

Q. *What if I feel the mixers aren't right for my group?*
A. There are many mixers in this book. Choose one or two from another evening plan and adapt it to suit your group's needs.

Q. *How important are the decorations and music to the evening?*

A. You may have a very successful evening without these extras. Making the effort to add a few decorations or to play a few tunes in keeping with the theme will tell your guests that you want them to have an enjoyable time.

Q. *I'd like to host the evening, but I think there is too much food preparation for one person to handle. How do I get around this problem?*

A. Delegate! Ask your visitors to supply a side dish, breads, beverages, or dessert. Most guests will be happy to contribute something to an evening you've worked hard to prepare.

Q. *How should I use the Related Scripture section?*

A. You may read the Scripture before the meal as a meditation. Or you may use it as a starting point for the discussion. Finally, you may want to save the Scripture passage until after the discussion to tie important points together.

Q. *How should I use the discussion questions?*

A. Choose the questions that work best for your group, and don't feel compelled to use every question. Substitute your own questions if they will help the discussion. The point is to get everyone talking in a comfortable, free manner.

Supper Club should provide you and your guests with a wonderful evening of fellowship and fun. Happy dining!

FIRST-CENTVRY CHVRCH EVENING

Theme

Most "early church" meals tend to revolve around the themes of secrecy and persecution. But for this evening the emphasis is placed more firmly on what Christians did when they were together rather than on how the world treated them.

For this event, send handwritten invitations on parchment-style stationery. Roll them up like scrolls and tie them with plain string. Make sure they are delivered in person, with some formality. (Children will likely enjoy the role of couriers.)

Sample invitation:

Grace and peace from the Lord Jesus Christ to your house. That part of Christ's church that meets in _____'s house would be honored by your presence with us for an agape meal and worship of our Lord on _____(date). Please come at sundown (or when your sundial reaches VI).

Dress

Have your guests create and wear costumes of the kind that might have been worn by New Testament–era people.

Decorations

Keep the lighting subdued. Because furniture was sparse, you may choose to spread blankets or sheets on the floor of your living room and have your guests talk and dine there. Candles and oil lamps would be appropriate and historically accurate decorations. Draw ancient symbols of the faith (such as the fish) on posterboard or newsprint and hang them on the walls.

Music

Rather than play recorded music (there aren't too many "Hits from Bible Times" CDs!), you may want to sing hymns, accompanied by basic instruments, such as a recorder, finger cymbals, or a small stringed instrument. Provide each guest with a lyric sheet, especially if you want to try out some unfamiliar tunes.

Mixers and Games

Who Am I?

Read the following clues about New Testament personalities to your guests and have them guess the answers. For a more competitive atmosphere, divide the group into two teams and have them compete for points. Award two points for a correct answer, but subtract one point for an incorrect answer.

1. After I met Jesus, I gave half my possessions to the poor and gave back to those I had cheated four times what I owed them. (Zacchaeus)
2. In the eighth chapter of Acts, you'll read how I helped the Ethiopian eunuch find Christ. (Philip)
3. I wrote the shortest book of the New Testament. (John)
4. Because my slave Onesimus ran away from me, Paul wrote me a letter urging me to take him back in a loving way. (Philemon)
5. I was a kind woman who did many things for the poor. When I became ill and died, Peter helped bring me back to life. (Dorcas or Tabitha)
6. I was a king who accused Paul of trying to turn me into a Christian. (Herod Agrippa)

7. I offered to make tents for Moses and Elijah when they appeared with Jesus in the transfiguration. (Peter)
8. Paul refused to take me on his second missionary journey, so I ended up going with Barnabas. (John Mark)
9. I was the older sister of Mary and Lazarus, and I tended to worry about details when guests came to my home. (Martha)
10. I was a polished orator who needed to hear the rest of the story about Jesus from Priscilla and Aquila before my message really made an impact. (Apollos)
11. Paul wrote his last letter to me, encouraging me to hold to the faith during the trials that would come. (Timothy)
12. According to John's account, I was the first person to notice that the stone had been rolled away from Jesus' tomb. (Mary Magdalene)

New Testament Scavenger Hunt

Notify guests before they arrive that they should bring an NIV Bible or New Testament (or any translation that is popular at your church—just make sure everyone has the same version). Then give them this list of twelve New Testament mystery words. They are to find the one verse in the New Testament in which each particular word is found (Old Testament citations don't count). Remember, no concordances!

1. Kidron Valley (John 18:1)
2. Malta (Acts 28:1)
3. the Stone Pavement (John 19:13)
4. Barak (Heb. 11:32)
5. Jannes and Jambres (2 Tim. 3:8)
6. Apollyon (Rev. 9:11)
7. Pool of Siloam (John 9:7)
8. Urbanus (Rom. 16:9)
9. Euodia (Phil. 4:2)
10. Baal (Rom. 11:4)
11. Gadarenes (Matt. 8:28)
12. bandits (2 Cor. 11:26)

The Gift of Hospitality

This mixer is a little more serious than the other two, but it should make your guests feel at home. Remember that people in Bible times were "experts" at hospitality—or were expected to be. The treatment Jesus received in the home of the Pharisee (Luke 7:36–50) was rude because the host did not extend to Jesus what was considered common courtesy (water for dusty feet, a welcoming gesture, oil for the guest's head). Greet each of your guests in a warm and personal way. Tell them you are glad they are under your roof and that you pray they will find it a place of hospitality. You might have a discussion when everyone arrives, using the passage from Luke as a starting point to brainstorm all the ways you might make guests feel welcome in your homes. (After all, most people have stopped washing the feet of their guests, no matter how distinguished their visitors might be!)

• • • • • • • •

Menu

Consider preparing hot towels for your guests, especially if you decide to serve the Damascus hens, as your guests will then be eating with their fingers. You will need two clean towels for each guest. Just before the meal, wet half the cloths in hot water, wring them out well, roll them up individually, and zap them in the microwave. Experiment to get the right time for the number of towels you are doing. They can get quite hot! But a very warm, damp towel can be a particularly unexpected treat. Repeat following the meal.

Beverage: Water or grape juice

Appetizers: Rye bread and rolls; simple green salad with vinegar and oil; various whole fruits (the more, the better)

Main Dish: Damascus hens. Prepare one cornish game hen for each guest. Stuff and roast according to directions. Use an herb stuffing, but add snipped dried apricots or dates to the stuffing. Serve the hens whole.

Side Dish: Parsleyed Carrots
Ingredients
3 pounds pared carrots
1 1/2 tablespoons salt
1 teaspoon Accent

Sauce
1 1/4 cups brown sugar, packed
1 teaspoon salt
1/2 teaspoon Accent
7 tablespoons hot water
1/2 cup butter

For serving
2 cups finely chopped fresh parsley

Quarter the carrots in 3-inch lengths, then cook in boiling water to which you have added the salt and Accent. Cook for 15 minutes, during which time the carrots should become barely tender.

Meanwhile, butter a roasting/serving pan. Drain the carrots and arrange them in the pan. In a saucepan, mix the brown sugar, salt, and Accent with the 7 tablespoons of hot water and cook for about 3 minutes, until a thin syrup is formed. Add the butter, and as soon as it has melted, pour the mixture over the carrots. Bake at 400° for about 30 minutes, basting often. Serve with the chopped parsley, which guests can use to taste.

Dessert: A variety of fruits—apples, pears, berries, dates

Alternate Main Dish: Lamb Stew
Ingredients
3 pounds lamb cut into stew pieces

2 quarts water
1/2 cup chopped onion
1 small bay leaf
2 teaspoons salt
1 whole clove
1/2 teaspoon rosemary
1/2 teaspoon garlic powder
3 teaspoons Worcestershire sauce
Bisquick mix made up according to directions for dumplings
1/2 cup finely minced parsley

Place stew meat in large kettle and cover with the water. Add all the seasonings *except* the Worcestershire sauce and parsley. Bring to a boil, cover, and simmer very gently until the meat is tender—about 1 hour. Remove the bay leaf and add the Worcestershire sauce. After mixing well and adding the parsley, continue to simmer while you make the dumpling mix.

Bring the stew back to a boil, drop the dumplings into the liquid by teaspoonfuls, and cook for 10 minutes uncovered, then cover tightly and cook for 10 more minutes.

Use spatulas to lift out the dumplings and place them on a separate platter. Check the stew to make sure the sauce is thick and hearty. If necessary, add some flour and water paste to thicken it. Serve in large individual bowls, ladling the stew over the dumplings. Encourage the guests to dip their rolls into the gravy. The only utensils should be spoons.

● ● ● ● ● ● ● ●

Related Scripture

They devoted themselves to the apostles' teaching and to the fellowship, to the breaking of bread and to prayer. Everyone was filled with awe, and many wonders and miraculous signs were done by the apostles. All the believers were together and had everything in common. Selling their possessions and goods, they gave to anyone as he had need. Every day they continued to meet together in the temple courts. They broke bread in their homes and ate together with glad and sincere hearts, praising God and enjoying the favor of all the people. And the Lord added to their number daily those who were being saved.

Acts 2:42–47

This brief description should stimulate a lively discussion of the contrasts between the early church and the experience of Christians today.

Discussion Questions

Icebreakers

1. What do you think would have been the most difficult part of being a first-century Christian?
2. Besides Jesus, what New Testament personality do you admire most? Why?
3. What book of the New Testament has been the most meaningful to you?
4. Throughout the centuries many Christian groups have attempted to model their fellowship and worship on the descriptions of the first-century church. Why do you think this model is so appealing?
5. If you were transported in time back to a first-century fellowship, how do you think you would fit in? What changes would you have to make?
6. Have you seen or read of someone who recently gave away his or her possessions?

Getting Serious

7. Is it really possible for Christians to return to the lifestyle of the first-century church? What would prevent such a return from happening?
8. Which of the qualities described in the passage above are lacking in the life of most churches?
9. How tightly do you hold on to your possessions?

10. Why do you suppose the lifestyle of these early Christians daily attracted new followers?
11. Do you believe, as author Ron Sider has suggested, that we are rich Christians in an age of hunger—in other words, that we Christians in the West have indulged ourselves in a materialistic lifestyle while showing indifference to the needs of most of the world?
12. What can your small group or church do to cultivate the gift of hospitality?

Wrap-up

Guests may choose to continue singing hymns, or they may want to end the evening with a time of prayer together. The theme of the prayer time may be suggested by the conversation and fellowship that occur, but also encourage guests to pray specifically for one another.

Medieval Quest Evening

Theme

As you invite guests, tell them that they are coming together to share what they've experienced during their "quests," that is, their faith journeys in life, and to encourage each other to continue in these quests.

Dress

Guests are to dress up like adventurers or characters from quests. Their choices do not have to be limited to medieval times. Here are some examples: knights, Indiana Jones, Robin Hood and his men, fair maidens, Huckleberry Finn, Marco Polo, kings and queens, jesters, a unicorn, a dragon, a crusader.

Decorations

Send out invitations that have a medieval look. Any decoration that gives your home the look of a Middle Ages castle would be ideal. Borrow replicas of medieval shields and swords, or try making them yourself from cardboard. Buy plates, napkins, and a disposable tablecloth decorated with unicorns or knights. Decorate your house with gold and silver streamers, balloons, and foil confetti. Add prints or pictures of kings, queens, fair maidens, dragons, and so on.

Music

Many recordings of medieval compositions, including morality plays, music dramas, and Gregorian chants, are available at larger record stores and libraries.

Mixers and Games

Questers' Tournament

This series of games will require some preparation before the evening, so read the description of each contest carefully to see what items you'll need. It is preferable, but not absolutely necessary, to play these games outdoors.

Divide the group into two teams. Inform the participants that this tournament will consist of four different challenges: The Shooting Star, Get the Point, the Fair Lady Toss, and Share the Secret.

The Shooting Star. Pass out plastic children's bows and suction-cup arrows. Put a target (with numbers) up on the wall and have the teams shoot to see who can come closest to the bull's-eye. Operate on a point system, adding the numbers according to where the arrows stick.

Get the Point. Mark off a square in a room or in the yard for a fighting platform. Choose one champion from each team, and give each champion a handkerchief and a "sword" (a cardboard wrapping-paper roll). Each contestant should place the handkerchief around his or her belt or in a back pocket. They must then engage in a sword fight, the goal of which is to steal the other person's handkerchief. Instruct the champions that blows to the head will result in disqualification, but everything else is OK.

Fair Lady Toss. Have all the women stand in a row, facing the men, who also stand in a row. Give each man a rose. Each must toss the rose as close to his lady's feet as he can, without actually touching her feet. In the event of a tie, have a toss-off with a smaller rose.

Share the Secret. This is a variation of the popular board game Pictionary (where one person draws an object or concept and the others on the team guess what he or she is drawing). For this game, use a list of words or names pertaining to adventures or quests. Examples: the Holy Grail, unicorns, Robin Hood, Daniel Boone, Columbus, Indiana Jones, dragons, the Crusades, the Fountain of Youth, Huck Finn, the Vikings, Leif Eriksson, pirates, Kit Carson. Number the list. On "Go!" one member from each team must run up to the "word giver," get the first word, then run back and draw it until someone on the team guesses the word. Whoever guesses correctly must then run up to get the next word. The first team to guess all the words wins.

Scripture Hunt

Choose an appropriate (but not too easy!) Scripture verse and write it out on a piece of paper, then cut the paper verse into one- or two-word pieces. Number the pieces, then hide them around the house (and yard, if you wish), keeping track of your hiding places. Make a list of clues for the hiding places (behind a mirror: "If you find this piece, it will reflect well on you!"; under a piano bench or stereo: "The hills aren't the only things that are alive with the sounds of music!"; on a rose bush: "We rose to the occasion to hide this piece!"). Make two copies of your clue sheet.

Divide the group into two teams, then give each a clue sheet. Give the teams fifteen minutes to find all the puzzle pieces they can, using the clues. As each piece is found, the number should be called out so both teams can cross it off on the clue sheet. When all the pieces have been found, the two teams have sixty seconds to lay out the pieces and try to figure out the Scripture verse from the pieces they have. The winning team is the first one to recite the verse *exactly*.

If neither team comes up with the correct verse, they can have another thirty seconds to barter with each other for other pieces of the verse.

Coat of Arms

Gather the group around a table where you've put construction paper, crayons, glitter, stickers, and other craft items. Have them (individually or in couples) make coats of arms for themselves. You should have a coat of arms that you've done already as an example of what you want. Have them divide their crest into four parts: what they think of God; what they think of their relationships; what they like to do; and what they think of themselves.

● ● ● ● ● ● ● ●
Menu

Have one couple or two guests bring a stew. Another couple should come with sliced or prepared meat (roast beef, corned beef, ham, summer sausage, chicken wings). You should supply breads (*unsliced* rye, wheat, pumpernickel), raw vegetables, almonds, and chunks of cheese. Furnish such beverages as mulled cider, water with lemon, and tea. Other guests should bring pastries and puddings.

If possible, announce the meal with a horn blast of some sort. Each guest should be given a trencher—a large slab of heavy bread that will serve as a plate. Explain that there are no forks—only spoons and knives. Meats and finger foods are to be eaten with the hands. The best of table manners is expected and the height of courtesy is to help someone else eat. For example, men help women, guests help host, and so on.

● ● ● ● ● ● ● ●

Related Scripture

> Those who hope in the LORD will renew their strength. They will soar on wings like eagles; they will run and not grow weary, they will walk and not be faint.
>
> Isaiah 40:31

Our journey on earth is filled with perils and hardships. This verse reminds us that God's strength is never exhausted. His power will enable us to rise above life's difficulties.

Discussion Questions

Icebreakers

1. What is your favorite adventure movie, book, or story?
2. Describe the best adventure you had as a child.
3. What do you find most admirable about life in medieval times? Explain your answer.
4. At what time in your life were you the most adventurous?
5. If you had to go on a quest—one that could be dangerous at times—which three people would you want to go with you? Why?
6. Have you ever felt as though a dream (aspiration) of yours had come true? Explain your answer.

Getting Serious

7. One of the greatest journeys in literature is that of Christian in *Pilgrim's Progress.* How would you describe where you are on your journey to the Celestial City?
8. Would you want to be offered the ability to see the future? Why or why not?
9. How has God renewed you on your spiritual journey recently?
10. How would you describe your daily preparation for your spiritual journey?
11. In what ways should your dreams be compatible with God's plan for your life?
12. What would you like to accomplish before your life is over?

Wrap-up

The King Who Does Not Lie

This game is based on an actual truth-or-dare game that was played during medieval feasts.

First, appoint the king (or queen). Give him or her a list of questions (different from the ones used in the discussion period). Tell those answering that they can either tell the truth or lie. The king must

determine whether the answer is true or not. If the king guesses correctly, the person must then do some act of chivalry (sing a song, recite
a poem, dance) as decided by the group.

Possible questions

How many traffic tickets have you received in the past twelve
  months?

What is your favorite meal?

Who is your favorite actor or actress?

If you had to move, what state would you choose for your new
  home?

What is your favorite piece of classical music?

What was the most useless birthday gift you ever received?

Do you trust your mate's (or girl/boyfriend's) driving?

What television commercial do you hate the most?

What is the best practical joke you ever pulled on someone?

What is your favorite sports team?

Who was your favorite teacher in high school?

1950s Evening

Theme

It's time to rock around the clock! The '50s are fondly remembered as America's golden era, a time when jobs were plentiful, families were happy and prosperous, and the future was bright. This evening will bring back memories of that time of innocence.

Dress

Guests should come in 1950s attire. Women might want to dress up as June Cleaver or Donna Reed, complete with apron, pearls, and high heels. For a younger look, ponytails and saddle oxfords would fit the bill. Men could wear letter jackets and sweaters, black leather, and/or jeans, complete with shades and loafers or high tops. Add a dab of Brylcream or slap on hair gel for a slicked-back look.

Decorations

Posters of hit movies from the decade will get noticed: *On the Waterfront, The Blackboard Jungle, Vertigo, The Ten Commandments, Ben Hur, The Bridge Over the River Kwai, From Here to Eternity.* You could drape your living room with crepe paper streamers and flowers to create a gym sock hop effect. Play videocassettes of popular television series, such as *I Love Lucy, Leave It to Beaver, Ozzie and Harriet,* and *Father Knows Best.*

Music

Rock and roll was just beginning. Play golden oldies by Elvis Presley, Little Richard, Buddy Holly, The Drifters, Chuck Berry, Fats Domino, Pat Boone, and Frankie Avalon. You can frequently buy inexpensive cassettes of 1950s hits at discount stores. Remember, too, that crooners were still popular as well. Hits by Frank Sinatra, Nat King Cole, Bobby Darin, and Tony Bennett will put your guests in a mellow mood.

Mixers and Games

Trivia Contest

Have guests play individually, in couples, or divide everyone into two teams. Ask the following questions. Award two points for a correct answer, but subtract one point for an incorrect guess.

1. What was the best-selling nonfiction book from 1952 to 1954?
2. What pitcher threw a perfect game in the 1956 World Series?
3. What was the name of the professor involved in a 1959 quiz show scandal?
4. What Cleveland Browns running back was named player of the year in 1957 and 1958?
5. Who recorded the 1957 hit "Tammy"?
6. What was the most popular show on television from 1952 to 1955?
7. What film featured Bill Haley and the Comets' hit "Rock Around the Clock"?
8. What South Carolina senator delivered a record twenty-four-hour filibuster against civil rights in 1957?
9. In what city did Wally and Beaver Cleaver live?
10. What 1955 hit brought fame to Elvis Presley?

11. What famed rock and roller died in a plane crash in Iowa in 1959?
12. What woman was *Time's* Man of the Year for 1952?
13. Who wrote the 1957 best-seller *Kids Say the Darndest Things?*
14. What did Roger Bannister accomplish on May 6, 1954?
15. What Illinois politician suffered consecutive defeats in presidential elections to Dwight Eisenhower?
16. The "kitchen debate" of 1959 featured what two world statesmen?
17. What couple was executed in 1953 for giving atomic weapons secrets to the Soviets?
18. Who played the pharaoh Ramses in the 1956 film *The Ten Commandments?*
19. What doctor perfected the vaccine that prevented outbreaks of polio?
20. What significance did the 38th parallel have in world affairs in the 1950s?
21. Whose 1954 Pulitzer Prize-winning autobiography was titled *The Spirit of St. Louis?*
22. What 1958 best-seller was penned by an unknown author named Grace Metalious?
23. What country took part in the 1952 Summer Olympics after a forty-year absence?
24. What country offered Albert Einstein its presidency in 1952?
25. Who wore mugshot number 7089 after his 1956 arrest in Montgomery, Alabama?

Answers
1. The Holy Bible, Revised Standard Version
2. Don Larson
3. Charles Van Doren
4. Jim Brown
5. Debbie Reynolds
6. *I Love Lucy*
7. *The Blackboard Jungle*

8. J. Strom Thurmond
9. Mayfield
10. "Heartbreak Hotel"
11. Three possible answers: Buddy Holly, the Big Bopper, and Richie Valens
12. Queen Elizabeth II
13. Art Linkletter
14. He was the first person to run the mile in under four minutes.
15. Adlai Stevenson
16. Vice President Richard Nixon and Soviet Premier Nikita Khrushchev
17. Ethel and Julius Rosenberg
18. Yul Brenner
19. Dr. Jonas Salk
20. It became the partition between North and South Korea after the end of the Korean War.
21. Charles Lindbergh
22. *Peyton Place*
23. The Soviet Union
24. Israel
25. Martin Luther King Jr.

What's My Line?

You can create interesting variations on this popular game show from the 1950s. Have a contestant leave the room and think of an obscure occupation. He or she should write this odd line of work on a piece of paper, come back into the room, and hand the paper to a person who has volunteered to serve as host of the show. Then the other guests ("panelists") must try to guess this person's occupation. There are a few restrictions. First, each guest may ask only one question per turn. All guests must ask a question before a panelist can have another turn. Second, the questions must be phrased in such a way that the only response can be a yes or a no. Third, only twenty questions are allowed. Once the round is over, select another guest to come up with a baffling occupation.

For variety, have the mystery guest choose a famous personality from the 1950s. Have panelists try to guess his or her identity in twenty questions or less.

Drawing Droodles

This '50s fad originated with TV writer Roger Price. A "droodle" is a strange-looking line drawing. Its meaning is not readily apparent until the caption is revealed. Many of your guests will undoubtedly have seen such drawings. Some of the more famous ones have captions like "Ship Arriving Too Late to Save a Drowning Witch," "Giraffe Standing in Front of a Window," and "Man with Sombrero Riding a Bicycle."

• • • • • • • •

Menu

Beverages: Root beer floats (black cows) or chocolate milk shakes. Use soda glasses or tall drinking glasses, long spoons, straws, and maraschino cherries for these favorites. For the floats put a scoop of ice cream in the glasses and fill with root beer.

To make the shakes, put 2 cups of milk, 1/2 cup of chocolate sauce, and 4 big scoops of vanilla ice cream in a blender. Blend 10–15 seconds and check for thickness.

Main Dish: Red Glazed Pork Chops
8–12 pork chops
Marinating Sauce
2 cups soy sauce
1 cup water
1/2 cup brown sugar
1 tablespoon dark molasses
1 teaspoon salt

Mix and bring to a boil. Let cool. Put chops in pan and pour sauce over them. Let stand in refrigerator overnight. Take out of sauce next day and bake in pan covered tightly with foil at 350° to 375° for 2 hours. While chops are cooking, prepare red sauce.

Red Sauce
1/3 cup water
1 14-ounce bottle ketchup
1 14-ounce bottle chili sauce
1/2 cup brown sugar
1 tablespoon dry mustard

Bring all ingredients to a slight boil. After chops are tender, dip in red sauce and return to oven (at 350°) for another 30 minutes or until slightly glazed. Chops may be placed on a grill instead of in oven.

Standby: Hamburgers on the grill. Provide toppings such as cheese, lettuce, onions, tomatoes, ketchup, mustard, and mayonnaise. If you have a fryer, cook up french fries and onion rings.

Dessert: Brownies with vanilla ice cream and chocolate sauce. Sundaes with chocolate, strawberry, or butterscotch toppings will also be popular with guests. More ambitious hosts may want to try the following recipe for whoopie pies.

Ingredients
1 cup cocoa
4 1/2 cups sifted flour
2 cups sugar
1 cup shortening
2 teaspoons baking soda
2 teaspoons salt
2 teaspoons vanilla
2 egg yolks (save the whites for filling)
1 cup sour milk (add tablespoon of lemon juice or vinegar to cup
    of regular milk and let stand for 5 minutes)
1 cup hot water

Combine all the ingredients. Mix thoroughly. Drop by generous spoonfuls onto greased cookie sheet. Bake at 400° for 8 minutes. Cool before filling.

Filling
  2 egg whites—stiffly beaten
  1 1/2 cups shortening
  2 teaspoons vanilla
  4 tablespoons flour
  4 cups confectioners sugar

Beat egg whites with electric mixer. Gradually add remaining ingredients, beating thoroughly at medium speed after each addition. Fill the cookies and put them together sandwich-style. There's plenty of filling—don't skimp.

● ● ● ● ● ● ● ●

Related Scripture

Brothers, I do not consider myself yet to have taken hold of it. But one thing I do: Forgetting what is behind and straining toward what is ahead, I press on toward the goal to win the prize for which God has called me heavenward in Christ Jesus.

Philippians 3:13–14

This verse reminds us that the "best times" are yet to come. People often imagine that the happiest times of life are ones that have occurred in days past, and that is part of the reason for the enduring popularity of the 1950s. But the apostle Paul reminds us to set our sights on the goal that lies ahead of us.

Discussion Questions

Icebreakers

1. Why do people look back on the 1950s as such a fun, innocent era?

2. What influences from the 1950s still affect our culture today?
3. What were the key events in your parents' lives during this decade?
4. If you could witness one event from the 1950s, what would it be?
5. In what ways did your family resemble—or seem removed from—the television families of the Nelsons, the Ricardos, and the Cleavers?
6. What person personifies the '50s to you? Why?

Getting Serious

7. What are the dark memories of the 1950s that many people tend to forget? (Examples: threat of atomic warfare, Communist scares and McCarthyism, segregation and racial violence.)
8. In what ways were our parents better off in the 1950s than we are today?
9. How have women's roles and goals changed since the 1950s? Do you think these changes are for the better or worse?
10. What made life easier—or tougher—for parents in the 1950s?
11. In what ways have the moral standards of our country changed since the 1950s?
12. How do you think people will remember our society forty years from now?

Wrap-up

Divide the guests into two teams. Each team is to write a 1950s-style commercial for some product that is popular today. Have teams act out their finished script.

1960s Evening

Theme

Relive the groovy days of the 1960s in this mind-bending, psychedelic evening of food and fun. Many of your guests will enjoy talking about their memories of this wild, turbulent time in our history.

Dress

Encourage guests to dress up in bell-bottoms, fringe vests, psychedelic or tie-dyed shirts, wide belts, round, wire-rim glasses (the John Lennon look), headbands—anything that gets them in the groove.

Decorations

Use your imagination. How about a Peter Max poster? Or crepe paper flowers? Try hanging beads in the entrance to several rooms. Overstuffed pillows on the floor are a nice touch, as are Chianti bottles with candles placed in them. Put blinking Christmas tree lights in a fishbowl-size frosted globe. Get those beanbag chairs out of the attic. For the all-out '60s atmosphere, burn incense or borrow a lava lamp. You might be able to buy some of these relics in a secondhand shop, or you might be able to make them yourself inexpensively.

Music

Music—especially rock music—dominated youth culture in the 1960s. Borrow or purchase music of the most popular acts of the era. Don't forget the Beatles, Simon and Garfunkel, the Byrds, the Mamas and Papas, the Monkees, the Doors, the Supremes, the Temptations, Herman's Hermits, the Lovin' Spoonful, and Paul Revere and the Raiders.

Mixers and Games

Name Game

As guests arrive, have them adopt a name. They can become a famous personality from the 1960s, or they can use a more generic "counterculture" name. Have guests write their new identities on name tags you have provided. They can choose from this list or think of their own.

Sunflower	Peace Child	Harmony
Moondog	Ringo	HAL 9000
Donovan	Tiny Tim	Twiggy
Broadway Joe	Lady Bird	Melanie

Express Yourself

Write out the following slang expressions on a sheet of poster board. Have each guest pick a phrase. During the evening, he or she has to use it at least five times during conversation.

"freaky"	"sock it to me"	"far out"
"dig it"	"groovy"	"cool"
"what a trip"	"flower power"	"heavy"
"peace, man"	"don't trust anyone over 30"	"let it be"
"come together"	"no, we won't go"	"spaced-out"
"burn, baby, burn"		

Trivia Challenge

As guests wait for the meal, pose the following trivia questions:

1. With what country did the U.S. break relations on January 3, 1961? (Cuba)
2. What thirty-five-year-old, with a record of fifteen arrests, became the youngest person to garner the Nobel Peace Prize? (Martin Luther King Jr.)
3. What 98-cent piece of rubber bounced into people's lives in 1965? (Wham-o Super Ball)
4. What did Ronald Reagan become in 1962? (a Republican)
5. What rock opera opened on Broadway on April 29, 1968? (*Hair*)
6. Where were the 1968 Olympic Games held? (Mexico City)
7. What island was seized by Native American activists in 1969? (Alcatraz)
8. What was the number of the Apollo mission that landed on the moon? (11)
9. What politician's strong showing in the 1968 New Hampshire primary forced Lyndon Johnson out of the presidential race? (Eugene McCarthy)
10. What two teams played in the first Super Bowl? (Green Bay Packers and Kansas City Chiefs)
11. In 1968, who became the first black woman elected to Congress? (Shirley Chisholm)
12. Who was John F. Kennedy's Attorney General? (brother Robert F. Kennedy)
13. What Beatle was rumored to have been killed and replaced by a look-alike? (Paul McCartney)
14. What musician electrified the masses at Woodstock with his unorthodox rendition of the "Star-Spangled Banner"? (Jimi Hendrix)

Note: Ambitious groups may want to play a more challenging board game like the various Trivial Pursuit games aimed at baby boomers.

Other Games

Guests will get a kick out of playing old board game standbys like Battleship, Operation, and Life. Younger groups may really enjoy playing a game of Twister—that is, if you can find someone who still owns the game! If you are going outdoors, why not play croquet or lawn darts? Another possibility is the Trust Walk. Blindfold one or two people and lead them with verbal instructions around a course of obstacles. Then have these blindfolded guests fall backwards into someone's arms at unexpected moments.

● ● ● ● ● ● ● ●

Menu

Appetizers: Cheese fondue
Ingredients
1 cup apple juice
2 cloves garlic, minced
2 cups (8 ounces) shredded Swiss cheese
4 tablespoons flour
2 cans (10 3/4 ounces each) condensed cheddar cheese soup
2 pounds bite-size wiener pieces

In a saucepan or fondue pot, simmer juice and garlic over low heat. Combine cheese and flour; gradually blend into juice. Heat until cheese melts, stirring occasionally. Blend in soup; heat until smooth, stirring constantly. To serve, spear wieners with a fork or toothpick and dip into fondue.

Of course, other appetizers will lend that '60s touch to your gathering without requiring so much work. Pour out a few bowls of trail mix or granola, sunflower seeds, or other crunchy health-food items. Or get out a box of Bugles, Fritos, or Ruffles (regular flavors—remember, ranch wasn't available back then!). Serve with California dip made from Lipton soup mix. For refreshments, offer drinks such as Fresca or Tang.

Main Dish: Vegetarian Quiche

Ingredients

1 piecrust, baked for 10 minutes

3 eggs, slightly beaten

2 cups warm half-and-half

1/2 teaspoon salt

pinch of pepper

3/4 cup grated Swiss cheese (Baby Swiss preferred)

1 cup cooked, well drained vegetables (sautéed onions and mushrooms, spinach, or asparagus are all nice. If desired, add 6 slices of cooked bacon to the mix.)

Combine eggs, half-and-half, salt, and pepper. Spread cheese evenly over crust, then spread vegetables on cheese. Pour milk and egg mixture over all. Place on cookie sheet. Bake at 350° for 30 minutes or until set. To test quiche, insert knife off center. If it comes out clean, the quiche is ready. Quiche must stand for 10 minutes before cutting. Serves six to eight people.

Alternate Main Dish: Tuna-Noodle Bake

Ingredients

3 cups (6 ounces) uncooked noodles or macaroni

1 package (10 ounces) chopped spinach or cut asparagus

2 cans (6 1/2 ounces each) tuna fish, drained

1 cup (4 ounces) shredded Swiss or mild cheddar cheese

1 2/3 cups (13 fluid-ounce can) evaporated milk

2 eggs

1/4 teaspoon salt or seasoned salt

paprika

Preheat oven to 350°. Cook noodles as directed on package. Drain and arrange in ungreased 2-quart shallow casserole. Cook spinach as directed on package, drain, and arrange on noodles. Flake tuna and sprinkle over spinach; top with cheese. Combine milk, eggs, and salt; beat well. Pour over casserole mixture. Sprinkle with paprika. Bake, uncovered, 30 to 40 minutes or until center is set. (Makes 5–6 servings. For larger groups, you may want to prepare a double portion.)

Dessert: Chocolate Mousse
Ingredients
8 ounces semi-sweet chocolate (chips are fine)
3 tablespoons unsalted butter
1/4 cup strong coffee
1/2 cup sugar
2 large eggs (separated)
2 cups heavy cream
1 cup heavy cream for garnish (optional)

Melt chocolate and butter in top of double boiler over barely simmering water. Meanwhile, over low heat, heat sugar and coffee until sugar dissolves. Add coffee to smoothly melted chocolate, stirring until blended. Add egg yolks one at a time until thoroughly blended. Remove from heat, allow to cool slightly. In a separate bowl, beat egg whites until stiff. Then whip cream and grently fold into egg whites. Slowly pour chocolate down side of egg-white/cream bowl and gently fold together. Spoon into serving bowl or individual containers. Chill several hours. Garnish with extra whipped cream before serving. Serves eight.

● ● ● ● ● ● ● ●

Related Scripture

There is a right time for everything:
A time to be born, A time to die;
A time to plant;
A time to harvest;
A time to kill;
A time to heal;
A time to destroy;
A time to rebuild;
A time to cry;

A time to laugh;
A time to grieve;
A time to dance;
A time for scattering stones;
A time for gathering stones;
A time to hug;
A time not to hug;
A time to find;
A time to lose;
A time for keeping;
A time for throwing away;
A time to tear;
A time to repair;
A time to be quiet;
A time to speak up;
A time for loving;
A time for hating;
A time for war;
A time for peace.

Ecclesiastes 3:1–8 TLB

You might want to read this passage aloud, then play the 1960s tune "Turn, Turn, Turn!" by the Byrds, which is based on this Scripture. Ask your guests what they think the passage/song is saying. What does this passage mean to them now compared to when they first heard the song?

Discussion Questions

Icebreakers

1. What was your favorite television show from this period?
2. What important national or world events from the '60s are most vivid in your memory?
3. Who was your best friend during this decade?
4. What was your favorite song?
5. What is the strangest article of clothing you wore during this period?

6. What church did you or your family attend during the 1960s?

Getting Serious

7. What were the big ideas of the '60s?
8. What significant events happened in your life (or in the life of your family) during the 1960s?
9. What evidence did you see of a generation gap in your family?
10. What events during this time had an impact on your spiritual development?
11. As you look back, how was God at work in your life during this time?
12. How did God become meaningful to you during this time?
13. How were the '60s helpful or harmful to you as a person?

Wrap-up

Afterward, sing folk songs—"If I Had a Hammer," "Puff, the Magic Dragon," and "Blowin' in the Wind" would be good selections—and see how well your guests remember the words. Then resume the games until everyone is ready to leave.

1970s Evening

Theme

OK, so maybe the '70s wasn't America's greatest decade. Yes, we had to endure Watergate, the end of Vietnam, long lines at the gas pumps, stagflation, and the hustle. But it was also a colorful decade during which the boomer generation came to maturity. Most of your guests will probably have enjoyable memories and plenty of stories to tell about their lives and times during this decade.

Dress

It's a tribute to polyester! Have everyone come in leisure suits, printed rayon shirts with flyaway collars, and platform shoes. Or some guests may opt for the more casual look of hiphugger, bell-bottom jeans and huarache sandals. Many of these hideous fashions are either still lurking in people's attics or basements or else they may be purchased at a local thrift store. Wear old campaign buttons from the period. If you're lucky, you might have an old WIN (Whip Inflation Now) button from President Ford's days in office.

Decorations

Black lights and black light posters (velvety, psychedelic prints painted with fluorescent colors) will give a certain early '70s authenticity to your evening. If you can get your hands on a disco ball (a multi-faceted, mirrored sphere that spins and reflects dots of light all over the room) or a strobe light (a rapidly blinking light), you will be able to recreate perfectly that mid-'70s high school dance atmosphere. Many Hollywood memorabilia stores sell old movie posters. You may want to buy several that advertise the biggest cinematic hits of the decade: *The Godfather (I* and *II), Rocky, The Sting, Animal House, Jaws,* and *Star Wars.*

Music

Have your guests bring their favorite tunes from the '70s. You will want to have on hand the disco sounds of the BeeGees, Donna Summer, and K.C. and the Sunshine Band as well as the rock sounds of the Doobie Brothers, BTO, Kansas, and Elton John. Discount retailers usually stock inexpensive cassettes ($3.99–$4.99) with titles like "Rock Hits of the '70s" and "'70s Disco Classics." It may be possible to borrow these albums from your public library. *Note:* You cannot have a quality '70s party without a copy of the soundtrack from *Saturday Night Fever!*

Mixers and Games

Name Game

As each guest arrives, stick the name of a famous person from the '70s on his or her back. (Use regular name tags.) Have your guests walk around the room, asking each other questions that can be answered with a yes or no in an attempt to discover the name of the celebrity. (Sample questions: Am I a male? Am I in the entertainment industry?) Use the following names:

Richard Nixon	Anita Bryant	Princess Leia
Billy Carter	Mary Tyler Moore	Alan Alda
Carol Burnett	Jimmy Connors	Billie Jean King
Bobby Fischer	Chevy Chase	John-Boy Walton

Roger Staubach	Reggie Jackson	Cheryl Tiegs
Kareem-Abdul Jabbar	Kathy Rigby	Pete Rose
Olivia Newton-John	Goldie Hawn	Leonid Brezhnev
R2-D2	Mean Joe Greene	Howard Cosell
Patty Hearst	Donny Osmond	Wonder Woman
Farrah Fawcett-Majors	Laverne DeFazio	Jimmy Hoffa

Remember When?

If your guests are good sports, have them each bring three photographs or slides of themselves taken during the '70s. While you are waiting for supper, get out the slide projector or pass the photos around and take a humorous trip down memory lane.

Jeopardy Challenge!

Pit the men against the women for this brain-teasing test of '70s facts. Remember, they have to answer in the form of a question. Alternate questions between sides. If one side misses, the other team gets a chance to answer. Award two points for a correct answer, but deduct one point for a wrong one. High score wins.

1. Popular syndicated columnist and author of *The Grass Is Always Greener Over the Septic Tank* (Who is Erma Bombeck?)
2. Feminist leader, former Playboy Club waitress, and founder of *Ms.* magazine (Who is Gloria Steinem?)
3. The television series that depicted a big, close-knit family trying to survive during the Great Depression (What is *The Waltons?*)
4. The middle name of Walter Mondale, President Jimmy Carter's Vice President (What is "Fritz"?)
5. The actress who with Farrah Fawcett-Majors and Jaclyn Smith comprised the original cast of *Charlie's Angels* (Who is Kate Jackson?)
6. The Triple Crown winner in 1973, considered by many to be the greatest thoroughbred race horse ever (Who was Secretariat?)

7. The champion ice skater whose hairdo was copied by millions of American women in the mid-'70s (Who is Dorothy Hamill?)

8. The toothless fighter with multiple driving citations who shocked the world by defeating Muhammed Ali in 1978 (Who is Leon Spinks?)

9. The name of the Supreme Court ruling that in 1973 legalized abortion on demand (What is *Roe v. Wade?*)

10. The name of the actor who played "Meathead" Michael Stivic on TV's popular *All in the Family* (Who is Rob Reiner?)

11. The man that Democratic presidential nominee George McGovern dumped as his running mate and replaced with Sargent Shriver (Who is Thomas Eagleton?)

12. The name of the radical group that kidnapped newspaper heiress Patty Hearst (What was the Symbionese Liberation Army?)

13. The duet that recorded a smash #1 single in 1976 called "Don't Go Breaking My Heart" (Who are Elton John and Kiki Dee?)

14. The city where Elvis Presley died in 1977 (What is Memphis, Tennessee?)

15. The name of the religious cult in Guyana led by American Jim Jones whose members committed mass suicide in 1978 (What was the People's Temple?)

16. The mastermind behind the Watergate break-in who served more than four years in prison and who later published a best-selling autobiography called *Will* (Who is G. Gordon Liddy?)

17. The name given to the tent that housed doctors Hawkeye Pierce, B.J. Honeycutt, and Frank Burns in the hit TV series *M*A*S*H* (What was "the Swamp"?)

18. Gerald Ford's running mate in the 1976 presidential election (Who is Bob Dole of Kansas?)

19. The Oscar-winning film about a down-and-out Philadelphia boxer who unexpectedly gets a shot at fighting the world champ (What is *Rocky?*)

20. The world's first "test-tube" baby, born in England on July 25, 1978 (Who is Louise Brown?)

• • • • • • • •

Menu

For most families the '70s were a tough time economically. Wage and price controls in the first part of the decade and double-digit inflation during the Carter years required simple, cost-conscious meals.

Main Dish: Meat Loaf
Ingredients
1 1/2 pounds ground beef or chuck (If you really want to be authentic, use Hamburger Helper!)
1 slice of bread
1/2 cup milk
1 egg
1 package Lipton onion soup mix

Mix bread, milk, egg, and soup mix. (You may need to soak bread a minute or two—then mix with a fork.) Add ground chuck and mix well. Shape into one big loaf or two small loaves. Place into a casserole dish sprayed with Pam. You can top the meat loaf with two slices of raw bacon. Bake at 350°–375° for 45 minutes to 1 hour. For an added touch, bake potatoes in the oven at the same time. Serves 6–8.

Alternate Main Dish: Chicken over Biscuits
Ingredients
2 cups cooked chicken
1 package frozen peas and carrots, cooked but not drained
3 ounces grated sharp cheddar cheese
1/2 cup white wine
1 can cream of chicken soup

Combine in a large Dutch oven or large skillet. Add salt and pepper, garlic or onion powder, if desired, and poultry seasoning if you wish. Heat and serve over biscuits. (Bisquick biscuits are quick and easy!)

Alternate Main Dish: "Beanie Weanies" (baked beans with wieners). Serve with cornbread. It's good and simple to make.

Salad: Jell-O can be used to make an inexpensive, colorful salad.

Dessert: How about good old-fashioned chocolate cake by Betty Crocker or Duncan Hines?

● ● ● ● ● ● ● ●

Related Scripture

The '70s was a decade dominated by political scandal. Because of Watergate, people lost faith in their elected leaders. Character and integrity became important issues.

For this reason you may wish to read Daniel 6. As a high-ranking government official, Daniel was known for his integrity and godliness. It is no surprise that his enemies combed carefully through his life looking for any dirt they could find! Psalm 15 is also a powerful statement about integrity.

Discussion Questions

After dinner, have an open forum. Choose questions that are appropriate for the group's spiritual maturity. If your group is made up of unchurched unbelievers, you may wish to guide the conversation and discuss the born-again movement that flourished in the mid-'70s. This topic can provide an excellent springboard to the gospel. If the group is composed primarily of Christians, use the discussion to encourage lifestyles of integrity as well as prayer for leaders.

Icebreakers

1. What are your most vivid memories of the '70s?
2. What was your favorite song/music/group?
3. What movies and/or TV shows did you enjoy most during this decade?

4. Why do you think polyester was so big during this decade?
5. Most clothing styles go in cycles. Do you foresee a time when leisure suits and platform shoes will make a comeback? Why or why not?
6. Who is your favorite personality from the '70s?
7. What aspects of the '90s will people make fun of twenty years from now?

Getting Serious

8. What were your thoughts in the midst of the Watergate scandal?
9. Why is our political system in such a mess today?
10. Do you think it is possible to have integrity and be a political figure? Why or why not?
11. How different are you now from the way you were in the '70s?
12. How much was God involved in your life during this decade?
13. President Carter and millions of other Americans in the 1970s claimed to be "born again." What does that concept mean to you?

Wrap-up

Close by playing the song "Dust in the Wind" by Kansas. Then discuss these questions:

1. What is the premise of this song?
2. Do you agree with the message of this song? Why or why not?
3. How is one who has been "born again" more than mere "dust in the wind"?

ALL ABOUT ME EVENING

Theme

It's your night! This lighthearted, nonthreatening evening is a perfect way to allow new people to get to know each other better. Guests will warm up to this opportunity to share little-known facts about their lives and to discuss the values in life that matter most to them.

This evening will require some information gathering before the event, so be sure to leave yourself plenty of time.

Dress

Encourage your guests to come in the kind of clothing they wore during the best year of their life. It might be their senior year of high school, the year they obtained a college degree, the year a child was born, and so on.

Decorations

Before the evening, call each guest and ask for a little-known fact about his or her life. Write these facts down on small pieces of posterboard. Statements might read something like "I shook hands with the President of the United States," "I have been to forty-one countries," or "My recipe for pound cake has won several prizes." Place these facts around the room and have each guest try to guess the persons described in the facts. Award a prize to the guest who gets the most right.

Music

Have your guests bring an album, cassette, or compact disc that typifies the kind of music they most enjoy listening to. Play a few songs or tracks from each guest's selection. While the music is playing, have the person who brought that music explain why he or she likes it and when he or she started liking it.

Mixers and Games

Vital Statistics

Have each guest write out answers to the following survey as you read the questions aloud. (They are modeled after the celebrity profiles that often appear in Sunday newspapers.) After people are finished, reread the first question and have each guest share the answer he or she wrote. Continue until all the questions have been answered. Encourage off-the-wall responses to keep the evening light. *Note:* Collect the responses after everyone is finished. Your guests don't know this yet, but you will be using their answers during the wrap-up for the evening.

Occupation:
Birth date:
Car/vehicle I drive:
Right now, I'm working on:
Book I'm recommending lately:
The last good movie I saw was:
As a child, I wanted to be:
The worst advice my parents gave me was:
My most irrational act was:
My favorite childhood memory is:
My favorite pig-out food is:

If I could be doing something else right now, I would:
People say behind my back:
The three words that best describe me: (example: smart, rich, and
  opinionated)

If . . .

Have guests respond to the following statements:

If I won $20 million, I would . . .
If I were President of the United States, the first thing I'd do would
  be . . .
If I had to spend the summer in another country, I'd choose to go
  to . . .
If I were asked to name the best movie of this year, I'd choose . . .
If I had one month to live, I would . . .
If I had athletic talent, I'd like to be . . .
If I could ban one commercial from the airwaves, it would be . . .
If I could do one thing over in my life, I would . . .

Talent Show

Have any willing guests display an unusual talent that they pos-
sess. Such stunning talent may include being able to wiggle one's nose
or ears, do the splits, whistle through one's nose, walk on one's hands—
the possibilities are endless. Afterwards, have everyone assign an
Olympics-style score to the performance (scale of 1–10). The person
with the highest total wins.

● ● ● ● ● ● ● ●

Menu

On a piece of paper, write in one column the names of the guests
who will be attending your party. In a second column, list the parts
of the meal you will be serving. For eight people, you may have two
main dishes, two side dishes, salad, breads, and two desserts. Match

up one person with each part of the meal. Then call that person to find out his or her favorite main dish, side dish, salad, bread, or dessert, depending on the pairings you have made. Then have one of the other guests prepare that part of the meal, taking note of any special requests. When finished, your chart may look like this:

Name	Favorite	To be prepared/ supplied by
Andrew	main dish: fried chicken	Deborah
Beverly	main dish: lasagna	Helen
Carl	side dish: scalloped potatoes	Garth
Deborah	side dish: broccoli with cheese sauce	Ed
Ed	salad: Caesar	Andrew
Felicia	bread: Italian breadsticks	Beverly
Garth	dessert: brownies	Felicia
Helen	dessert: cookie dough ice cream	Carl

Note: To avoid an abundance of leftovers, you may want to instruct guests to make smaller portions (serving 4–6), except perhaps the salad and bread suppliers.

● ● ● ● ● ● ● ●

Related Scripture

The man who loves God is known by God.

1 Corinthians 8:3

This verse reminds us that true knowledge of God comes only through loving him. We can know the right theological arguments, the most appealing Bible verses, and the best hymns, but they are no substitute for the knowledge of God that comes through prayer and study in the Word.

Discussion Questions

Icebreakers

1. What was your most embarrassing moment in front of a group of strangers?
2. What is your greatest accomplishment?
3. How many times has your picture appeared in a newspaper? Explain the circumstances.
4. Who is the most famous person you've ever met?
5. How have you changed since high school?
6. What would you like to be doing five years from now?

Getting Serious

7. What is the most serious crisis you've ever had to face?
8. What do you least like about yourself?
9. How would you describe your spiritual pilgrimage?
10. Why do you believe in God?
11. What is your biggest struggle right now?
12. How do you want to be remembered after your life is over?

Wrap-up

Newly Acquainted Game

Remember those responses you collected after the Vital Statistics mixer? You can reuse them in this test of memory. First, pair up the guests into couples—men with men, women with women would be ideal. Then have half of the partners leave the room while you ask the remaining contestants three of the Vital Statistics questions. These people must try to remember how their partners answered the questions earlier in the evening. (Of course, you have the answers in front of you!) Then call the other partners back into the room and have them respond to the questions again. Give five points for each correct match. Switch roles and repeat the process with the other partners, awarding ten points for correct answers. Give a prize to the winning partners.

Walt Disney Evening

Theme

Forget your troubles for a night and enjoy the magic of Disney.

Dress

Casual dress is appropriate for this evening. Guests may want to wear their favorite Disney paraphernalia or dress as a tourist. If they want to go way out, they could come as their favorite Disney character.

Decorations

If you have children, decorating may be easier since you may have many Disney products already. Posters, mirrors, stuffed animals, dolls, games, coloring books, and story books should be placed in your living or family room. Balloons will add a festive air. Rent or borrow a videotape of a Disney classic such as *Cinderella, The Little Mermaid, Mary Poppins,* or *Fantasia* and play it as guests start filing in.

Music

Many soundtracks to Disney movies are available on compact disc and cassette. If you don't own copies, try borrowing these recordings from neighbors, friends, or guests.

Mixers and Games

Head Game

As the guests come in, tape a character name to each one's forehead or back. They must find out who they are by asking the other guests yes or no questions. Here are some characters you may want to use:

Pongo	Tramp	Snow White
Belle	Mowgli	Donald Duck
Jiminy Cricket	Goofy	Ariel
Cinderella	Princess Jasmine	Baloo Bear
Minnie Mouse	Alice in Wonderland	Mickey Mouse
Pluto	Mary Poppins	Cruella DeVil
Pollyanna	Gaston	Thomasina
The Absent-Minded Professor	Old Yeller	The Love Bug

Charades

Write each of the film titles below on small strips of paper. Fold the strips and place them in a hat or bowl. Have a person choose a slip, then act out the name of the movie charade-style. The other guests will try to guess the title. Continue until everyone has had a turn to act out a title. You may want to review typical charade motions with your guests before you begin to play.

Pinnochio	*101 Dalmatians*
The Little Mermaid	*The Love Bug*
Beauty and the Beast	*Aladdin*
Fantasia	*Freaky Friday*
Bedknobs and Broomsticks	*The Jungle Book*
The Aristocats	*The Three Lives of Thomasina*
Sleeping Beauty	*Mary Poppins*
Bambi	*Song of the South*
Peter Pan	*The Great Mouse Detective*

Dumbo	*The Rescuers Down Under*
The Million-Dollar Duck	*Darby O'Gill and the Little People*
The Shaggy D.A.	*Escape to Witch Mountain*

Name That Tune

Play this game in the manner of the popular TV game show of the past. You will need a piano or electronic keyboard, plus a songbook of Disney tunes, or least someone who can play the basic melody without difficulty. In fact, you may want to jot down the first seven notes of each song and place them on index cards before the evening begins.

The game is played as follows: Divide your guests into two groups. Read a clue from the list below to one contestant from each side. The person on the right has the first opportunity to guess the tune. If the person feels confident, he or she offers to guess the tune in seven notes. The other contestant may then lower the bid by offering to guess the tune in six notes. The bidding continues until one contestant refuses to take the challenge of a lower bid or until the bidding reaches one note.

The person with the winning bid then listens as the piano/keyboard player plays the specified number of notes. If the answer is correct, his or her team wins two points. If the answer is incorrect, the other contestant gets to hear all seven notes and to offer a guess. If this answer is correct, the team wins two points. If the answer is incorrect, go on to two new contestants and a fresh tune. Continue until all the clues have been read.

1. Take a hint from the lady with the umbrella—this tune is very sweet. ("Just a Spoonful of Sugar")
2. According to Baloo in *The Jungle Book*, this is all you really need. ("The Bare Necessities")
3. Aladdin and Jasmine discover this while flying on their magic carpet. ("A Whole New World")
4. This invitation from *Beauty and the Beast* will make you feel at home. ("Be Our Guest")

5. Roger wrote this song about the woman who wanted to make fur coats out of puppies. ("Cruella DeVil")

6. According to this song, it's always better down where it's wetter. ("Under the Sea")

7. The sound of this song is something quite atrocious. ("Supercalafragilistic")

8. If you were down, Pollyanna would tell you to play this. ("The Glad Game")

9. If Mr. Bluebird is on your shoulder, you're going to have a wonderful day. ("Zippity Doo Dah")

10. This upbeat song will dwarf the task that's in front of you. ("Whistle While You Work")

11. In *Pinnochio,* Jiminy Cricket sings this lofty tune about finding your dreams. ("When You Wish upon a Star")

12. Why? Because we like you. ("Mickey Mouse Club Theme")

• • • • • • • •

Menu

Appetizers: Popcorn in small sacks; soft drinks in paper cups with straws

Main Dish: Minnie's Oven-Baked Chicken Breasts
Ingredients
 Boneless chicken breasts
 Butter or margarine
 Bread crumbs
 Parmesan cheese

Mix equal parts of bread crumbs and Parmesan cheese. Dip each chicken breast in melted butter and then roll in the bread crumbs and cheese mixture. Place in a baking dish. Bake at 350° for 1 hour.

Have guests contribute salads, side dishes, and bread to make the meal complete.

Alternate Main Dish: Under the Seafood Lasagna Rollups

Ingredients

6 lasagna noodles

1 15-ounce can Italian-style tomato sauce

Filling

1 8-ounce package Louis Kemp Crab Delights—flakes or
   chunks

1 cup ricotta cheese

1/4 cup grated Parmesan cheese

1 egg

1 tablespoon dried parsley flakes

1/4 teaspoon onion powder

Cook noodles according to directions. Rinse and drain well. Thoroughly combine filling ingredients. Spread 1/3 cup filling on each noodle. Roll tightly; place seam side down in 9-inch pan. Pour sauce over rollups. Bake at 375° for 30 minutes. (Serves 6.)

Dessert: Frozen bananas

Ingredients

Bananas

Milk chocolate chips

Chopped nuts

Sticks

Peel bananas and place on a stick. Place on a cookie sheet and freeze. Melt chocolate chips in a double boiler. Dip frozen bananas in chocolate and then roll in nuts. Return to freezer until serving time.

You may simply want to serve frozen Disney treats that can be found at most grocery stores.

● ● ● ● ● ● ● ●

Related Scripture

Blessed are the poor in spirit, for theirs is the kingdom of heaven.
Blessed are those who mourn, for they will be comforted.
Blessed are the meek, for they will inherit the earth.
Blessed are those who hunger and thirst for righteousness, for they will be
    filled.
Blessed are the merciful, for they will be shown mercy.
Blessed are the pure in heart, for they will see God.
Blessed are the peacemakers, for they will be called sons of God.
Blessed are those who are persecuted because of righteousness, for theirs is
    the kingdom of heaven.
Blessed are you when people insult you, persecute you and falsely say all kinds
    of evil against you because of me.
Rejoice and be glad, because great is your reward in heaven, for in the same
    way they persecuted the prophets who were before you.

                                                                    Matthew 5:3–12

Use this Scripture to further the discussion after you have completed the discussion questions. You may want to discuss each verse
separately and highlight how society would view that blessing and
what that blessing means for us as God's people.

Discussion Questions

Icebreakers

1. What is your favorite Disney movie, and why?
2. What is your earliest Disney memory?
3. Which land in Disneyland would you prefer to live in: Adven-
   tureland, Tomorrowland, Fantasyland, or Main Street USA?
4. Why do you think Disney has enjoyed such remarkable success
   in American society?
5. What admirable qualities can you find in most Disney films?
6. To what degree have children's movies become big business?

Getting Serious

7. What is one trial in your life that ended in the remarkable, happy way a Disney movie might?
8. What questionable ideas or values can be transmitted through children's films?
9. Walt Disney created Disneyland to be the "happiest place on earth." According to our society, what characteristics would the happiest place on earth have?
10. Reflect on the Beatitudes. How might the Disney definition of happiness differ from a Christian definition?
11. Where are the happiest places in your life?
12. In what ways do you keep God from writing the script for your life?

Wrap-up

Afterward, play Disney movies. Fast-forward to your favorite scenes. You may want to have each guest bring a favorite Disney movie.

INTERNATIONAL EVENING

Theme

Improved communications and travel have made even the most remote sections of the world accessible. But many Americans still have only faint ideas about how people in other countries live, work, play, and worship. An international evening allows your guests the opportunity of learning more about world cultures. More important, they can begin to learn ways of praying for and caring about people with physical and spiritual needs.

If your church has families from different countries, this fellowship idea is a great way of making them feel important and welcome.

Dress

When you invite your guests, you might want to encourage them to wear something that represents their heritage. When the group is gathered together, you could ask them how much their personal heritage has influenced their present lives. Or you might simply require that everyone wear an item of clothing that originates from another land. Have each guest describe why he or she selected that item of clothing.

Decorations

Posters featuring lush scenery from exotic vacation spots can be obtained cheaply and placed around the house. Art objects, figurines, paintings, blankets, and scarves from overseas will add color and generate discussion.

Music

Many larger record stores carry "world music." South African, Brazilian, and Caribbean music are good choices, for they often feature multiple instrumental arrangements, complex rhythms, and lively melodies. Add traditional songs from Germany, Ireland, Italy, and other European countries. You may be able to borrow such recordings from a library, or ask guests to bring along any international recordings they might own.

Mixers and Games

Where in the World Is Santiago, Carmen?

Obtain a current map and quiz your guests on their knowledge of present geography. One way is to ask what countries border a certain country. Another is to ask on which continent a certain country is found. Or let them brainstorm the answers to questions like: What countries make up Central America or Africa? Or give them the names of national capitals and have them guess the countries.

Global Scavenger Hunt

Designate each couple as a team. Have the teams identify objects in the house or around your neighborhood that come from other lands. If your house is lacking such objects, you may want to go to a dollar store or discount place and buy a few trinkets of foreign origin. Place them in inconspicuous locations in your home. Have each team tally their findings. Ask them also to identify as many foreign items as possible in their own surroundings. Then compare lists. The point is that most of us live surrounded by things made in other lands.

World Knowledge Quiz

Challenge your guests to determine correct answers for one or both quizzes.

Match the country with its official language:

Brazil _____	1. Khmer
Belize _____	2. Amharic
Cambodia _____	3. Spanish
Congo _____	4. Dutch
Ethiopia _____	5. Portuguese
Nicaragua _____	6. Sinhala
Oman _____	7. Italian
San Marino _____	8. English
Sri Lanka _____	9. Arabic
Suriname _____	10. French

Correct answers: Brazil—5; Belize—8; Cambodia—1; Congo—10; Ethiopia—2; Nicaragua—3; Oman—9; San Marino—7; Sri Lanka—6; Suriname—4

Match the country with its official currency:

Argentina _____	1. austral
Australia _____	2. rupee
Japan _____	3. zloty
Romania _____	4. dollar
Germany _____	5. krona
Ghana _____	6. mark
Mexico _____	7. yen
India_____	8. peso

(continued)

Sweden _____   9. cedi
Poland _____   10. lei

Correct answers: Argentina—1; Australia—4; Japan—7; Romania—10; Germany—6; Ghana—9; Mexico—8; India—2; Sweden—5; Poland—3.

● ● ● ● ● ● ● ●

Menu

I.

International Pot Luck
Appetizer: Alphabet soup
Beverages: Tea, water, soft drinks, coffee

Assign each couple two dish types to prepare—salad, meat, vegetable, dessert—so you will have two of each. They should use recipes from other countries.

II.

Main Dish: Fettuccini with Zucchini and Mushrooms
Ingredients
 2 tablespoons salt
 1 tablespoon olive oil
 12 ounces fettuccini noodles
 8 ounces fresh mushrooms, sliced
 1/4 cup butter or margarine
 1 1/4 pounds small zucchini, cut into 2 1/2-inch strips
 1 cup whipping cream
 1/4 to 1/2 cup butter or margarine (cut up)
 3/4 cup grated Parmesan cheese
 1/4 cup snipped Italian parsley
 salt and pepper

Bring large amount of water to boil with 2 tablespoons salt and the oil. Cook pasta for 7 minutes. Drain. In large skillet cook mushrooms in 1/4 cup butter over medium heat for 2 minutes. Add zucchini, cream, and 1/4–1/2 cup butter. Bring to boil. Reduce heat; cover and cook for 3 minutes. Add pasta to mushroom mixture in skillet. Add Parmesan and parsley, tossing till all is mixed. Season to taste with salt and pepper. Serve at once with loaf of bread.

To round out the meal, add a tossed salad or other green vegetable.

Dessert: Flan (Caramel Pudding)
Ingredients
1/4 cup sugar
4 eggs
1 14-ounce can sweetened condensed milk
1 cup water
1 teaspoon vanilla

Using a small, heavy saucepan, melt the sugar over low heat, stirring constantly. When the syrup turns smooth and golden brown, immediately pour the caramel into an oven-proof Bundt pan so that the syrup goes all the way around the circle. Set aside and turn on the oven to 350°.

In a mixing bowl, beat the eggs until frothy. Add the condensed milk, water, and vanilla and beat the mixture until smooth. Pour the custard into the caramelized mold. Place the mold in a larger pan into which you also add enough water to come halfway up the outside of the mold. This helps bake the custard very smoothly.

Bake for 1 to 1 1/4 hours, or until a knife inserted in the center of the custard comes out clean. Cool at room temperature, then refrigerate for at least 3 hours. Unmold the flan on a serving plate, garnishing the center with strawberries, grapes, or cherries.

• • • • • • • •

Related Scripture

Now there were staying in Jerusalem God-fearing Jews from every nation under heaven. When they heard this sound, a crowd came together in bewilderment, because each one heard them speaking in his own language. Utterly amazed, they asked: "Are not all these men who are speaking Galileans? Then how is it that each of us hears them in his own native language? Parthians, Medes and Elamites; residents of Mesopotamia, Judea and Cappadocia, Pontus and Asia, Phrygia and Pamphylia, Egypt and the parts of Libya near Cyrene; visitors from Rome (both Jews and converts to Judaism); Cretans and Arabs—we hear them declaring the wonders of God in our own tongues!" Amazed and perplexed, they asked one another, "What does this mean?"

Acts 2:5–12

This familiar passage describing the Pentecost reminds us that the gospel is intended for all nations. The Holy Spirit enabled each person present to hear the message of God's good news in his own tongue—a foreshadowing of the imminent spread of Christianity to many nations. We are reminded that God has a deep compassion for every person of every color, nation, and ethnic background.

Discussion Questions

Icebreakers

1. How many countries have you visited? If you have visited several, which ones were most interesting to you?
2. What country would you most like to visit someday? Why?
3. What is your most interesting encounter with a person or group from another culture?
4. What country seems the most mysterious or perhaps even threatening to you?
5. If you had to go abroad for five years, what skills would best serve you if you tried to find a job?
6. What is one foreign custom that you have a hard time accepting?

Getting Serious

7. How would a visitor from another country be received at your church?

8. What valid criticisms could be leveled about the way Americans live?

9. In what ways are you involved with the lives of people abroad?

10. What do you believe is the most critical problem the world is facing right now?

11. Do Christians place too much emphasis on overseas mission work, or not enough? Explain.

12. What is the most important thing *you* can do to improve our world?

Wrap-up

1. Have guests sing all the songs they can think of with foreign words. You may also choose songs with English words that clearly originated in another country.

2. Have each guest answer the question: When did your family come to America? If some guests don't know, have them relate as much as they are able about their national or ethnic background.

Great Literature Evening

Theme

All of us have favorite books that are close to our hearts, that have shaped our outlooks on life. This evening will give your guests an opportunity to discuss the authors and books that have meant the most to them.

Dress

Encourage your guests to come dressed as favorite characters from plays or novels. When they arrive, tell them that they shouldn't reveal their identities until later. Part of the fun of the evening will be guessing the characters. (See the first mixer below.)

Decorations

Elegance is the key! Place candles around the room. Display dust jackets or covers of famous books (perhaps also handcrafted or gilt-edged volumes). For a touch of class, serve sparkling white grape juice in wine glasses.

Music

Classical music is appropriate, especially music from the 17th and 18th centuries. These compositions will give your home a *Masterpiece Theatre* atmosphere.

Mixers and Games

Who Am I?

You can play this game in one of two ways. First, if your guests come dressed as famous characters in literature, you may have them try to guess one another's identity by asking questions that can be answered with a yes or no. Place a limit on the number of questions that may be asked. Give a quill pen or a bookmark to anyone whose identity isn't guessed.

The second variation is to tape the name of a famous literary character on the back of each guest as he or she arrives. Then everyone attempts to find out the name of his or her character by asking the other guests questions that can be answered with a yes or no. The first person to discover his or her identity wins a prize. Possible names:

David Copperfield
Captain Ahab *(Moby Dick)*
Ichabod Crane *(The Legend of Sleepy Hollow)*
Christian *(Pilgrim's Progress)*
Tess *(Tess of the D'Urbervilles)*
Jane Eyre
Winston Smith *(1984)*
Lancelot
Willie Loman *(Death of a Salesman)*
Becky Thatcher
Mr. Kurtz *(Heart of Darkness)*
Henry Fleming *(The Red Badge of Courage)*
Lady Macbeth
Cordelia *(King Lear)*
Jean Valjean *(Les Misérables)*
Hester Prynne *(The Scarlet Letter)*
Anne Shirley *(Anne of Green Gables)*
Odysseus
Othello
Ivan Karamazov
Madame Defarge *(A Tale of Two Cities)*

The Devil's Dictionary

The American writer Ambrose Bierce composed a satirical dictionary, complete with pithy, humorous definitions of common words. See if your guests can match Bierce's definitions with the proper words. (From Gyles Brandeth, *The Joy of Lex* [New York: Quill, 1983], 26–30.)

1. egotist

2. famous

3. opportunity

4. fashion

5. habit

6. mausoleum

7. alone

8. riot

9. positive

10. overwork

11. congratulation

12. debt

a. A despot whom the wise ridicule and obey

b. A person of low taste, more interested in himself than me

c. In bad company

d. Mistaken at the top of one's voice

e. A shackle for the free

f. Conspicuously miserable

g. A dangerous disorder affecting high public functionaries who want to go fishing

h. The civility of envy

i. An ingenious substitute for the whip and chain of the slave driver

j. The final and funniest folly of the rich

k. A popular entertainment given to the military by innocent bystanders

l. A favorable occasion for grasping a disappointment

(continued)

Answers: 1. b; 2. f; 3. l; 4. a; 5. e; 6. j; 7. c; 8. k; 9. d; 10. g; 11. h; 12. i

Bad Theatre

Divide your guests into two groups. Send each group to a different room of the house. Give each group five or six randomly selected objects. The "artists" are then to take fifteen minutes to write a short play, incorporating those objects into the narrative. Everyone in the group must say at least one line. Subjects can be light and humorous or deeply philosophical! Convene both groups after the fifteen minutes and have them perform their works.

● ● ● ● ● ● ● ●

Menu

Main Dish: Flank Steak
Ingredients
2 pounds flank steak

Marinade
1/4 cup olive oil
3/4 cup red wine vinegar
1 package onion soup mix
1 teaspoon oregano

Place flank steak in plastic Jiffy bag. Add marinade, and let sit for 4 to 6 hours. Remove from bag and broil, 7 minutes on each side. Slice *thin* on the diagonal (across grain). (Serves 8 people.)

Side Dish: Mixed Vegetable Casserole
Ingredients
1 10-ounce package frozen broccoli spears
1 10-ounce package frozen cauliflower
1 10-ounce package frozen brussels sprouts
1 8-ounce package shredded cheddar cheese

1 can cream of mushroom soup
1 package seasoned croutons

Steam vegetables until tender. Arrange in casserole dish. Cover with mushroom soup (don't dilute with water). Cover casserole dish. Bake in oven at 350° for 30 minutes. Uncover and top with cheese and croutons. Place in oven until cheese is melted and croutons are slightly browned.

Complete the meal with a selection of bread and rolls.

Dessert: Cakes or pastries. Or have guests bring favorite desserts that they would like to share with the group.

● ● ● ● ● ● ● ●

Related Scripture

[King Josiah] went up to the temple of the LORD with the men of Judah, the people of Jerusalem, the priests and the prophets—all the people from the least to the greatest. He read in their hearing all the words of the Book of the Covenant, which had been found in the temple of the LORD. The king stood by the pillar and renewed the covenant in the presence of the LORD—to follow the LORD and keep his commands, regulations and decrees with all his heart and all his soul, thus confirming the words of the covenant written in this book. Then all the people pledged themselves to the covenant.

2 Kings 23:2–3

In this familiar Old Testament story, King Josiah discovered the Book of the Law gathering dust in the temple. He was deeply moved by what he read and led his nation in repentance back to God. Josiah's story reminds us that the most important book we can read is the Bible. All the great works of literature pale in significance to the eternal truths found in God's Word.

Discussion Questions

Icebreakers

1. What is the first book you remember reading or being read to you as a child?
2. How much time do you spend reading during the week?
3. If you were marooned on a desert island, what three books would you want to have with you?
4. What is the longest book you have ever read?
5. What famous author or novel do you find boring or over-rated?
6. When have you read a book and seen a movie based on that book? Generally speaking, do you prefer reading a book or seeing a movie version of that book?

Getting Serious

7. What three contemporary authors do you think have something worth saying?
8. What character in the Bible do you identify with? Why?
9. Besides the Bible, what book written from a Christian perspective has made an impact on your life?
10. Why do you think Christians place such importance on daily Bible reading?
11. If someone close to you were to write a book about your life, what would be the title, the plot, the central characters, and the setting? Who would play you in a movie version?
12. Is there anything about your reading habits you would like to change? Explain your answer.

Wrap-up

Improving on a Masterpiece

Divide the group into two teams. Give each team a different list of ten titles of popular or classic works of literature. The teams are to rewrite the titles, but in such a way that they resemble the old ones. Examples: *The Catcher in the Rye* becomes *The Man Behind the Plate in a Field of Grain*; *The Caine Mutiny* becomes *The Walking Stick Overtaken by Sailors*; *War and Peace* becomes *Conflict and Tranquility*. When each team is finished, have guests read the clues to the others.

HIGH SCHOOL REUNION EVENING

Theme

This evening can be hosted in one of two ways: (1) it can be a general party for people who graduated from different schools in different years; (2) it can be a reunion for people who graduated from the same school and class. This second approach may take more work to pull off, but you will likely enjoy seeing friends that you haven't seen in years.

Dress

Tell guests to wear what they might have worn as seniors in high school. A letter jacket, football jersey, bell-bottoms, cheerleader's outfit, band uniform, or graduation cap and gown will help your guests get in the proper mood. Clothes that feature school colors are also a good idea. For the ultimate event, encourage the partygoers to dress up as if they were going to the prom. They don't have to rent tuxedos or buy expensive dresses, but the men should wear suits and the women should wear colorful dresses. Spouses should not forget to provide flowers for their dates!

Decorations

A high school dance in the gym can be recreated with paper streamers and flowers, appropriate music, and soft lights. Prepare a colorful backdrop and have the dates pose for pictures (have a camera ready). For a more day-in-the-life atmosphere, give the house a classroom feel. Set up desks and chairs, a podium for lecturing, a chalkboard or erasable board, cardboard painted or colored to look like lockers. Place a few yearbooks around the room.

Music

Have guests bring a cassette or compact disc that features music from their high school days. If they don't already own such music, they may be able to borrow it from a library or buy inexpensive collections of oldies from discount stores.

Mixers and Games

Most Likely to Succeed

Ask each guest to bring a senior portrait. Arrange the portraits on a table or bulletin board. Have each person also write down on a 3 x 5 index card a high school accomplishment and write his or her name on the back. Appoint one person to look at the backs of the cards and note the accomplishment that goes with each portrait. One at a time, let the guests try to line up the high school achievements with the pictures. Have the person holding the correct answers announce the number of correct and incorrect matches. Continue until all the accomplishments and portraits are correctly paired.

A fun variation is to guess the identities of celebrities from their high school portraits. Your library may have *Celebrity Yearbook* by Dan Carlinsky. It features many senior portraits ranging from the early 1900s to the present.

Travelogue

Place a large map of the United States (or, if necessary, the world) on a table. Ask each person to point out all the places he or she has lived since high school. To make this mixer more enjoyable, have the narrator relate a funny story or strange circumstance that occurred in each location.

Do You Remember?

Pose the following questions to your guests. Give one point to the first person who can recall an answer to these high school brain teasers. Award a specially prepared diploma to the person with the most points.

1. What was the name of your school newspaper?
2. Who was your school principal?
3. What was the name of the football field your team played on?
4. How many detentions did you serve during your high school years?
5. Name a classmate who had a locker next to yours.
6. Name a play that was performed at your school during your senior year.
7. Who taught Spanish (or French) at your school?
8. What person was, alphabetically speaking, the first in your class?
9. Who was the salutatorian (*not* valedictorian) of your senior class?
10. What team did your school play at your senior homecoming?
11. What was the theme of your high school prom?
12. Whom did you take (or go with) to your high school prom (or banquet)?
13. What was your personal nickname?
14. Who was president of your senior class?
15. What person was named most likely to succeed?
16. How much did a lunch cost at your school cafeteria?
17. At what time did the first class of the day begin?
18. How much did your class ring cost?
19. Who was your high school band instructor?
20. Who was the Vice President of the United States the day you graduated?

• • • • • • • •

Menu

School Cafeteria Nightmare

Have your guests line up single file near your kitchen. Give each person a tray and a disposable plate with dividers. Recruit two guests to dress up in white aprons and paper hats. As each guest passes by, have these servers plop the food in the proper section.

No special preparation is necessary. Buy institutional food (available at most larger grocery stores) and serve to your unsuspecting guests! As they eat, encourage them to recall the most horrifying meals they were served as teenagers.

Beverage: Cartons of white or chocolate milk. Serve at room temperature.
Main Dish: Salisbury steak (mystery meat) or canned spaghetti
Side Dishes: Tater Tots, macaroni and cheese, green beans
Dessert: Devil's food cake, peach cobbler, or Hostess SnoBalls

Prom Night Delight

If you want to serve your guests a more elegant meal, try this menu.

Beverage: Prom Punch
Ingredients
   1 quart cranberry juice cocktail
   1 6-ounce can orange juice
   1 6-ounce can lemonade
   2 7-ounce bottles ginger ale
   2 cups water

Main Dish: Chicken Bake
Ingredients
   1 can cream of mushroom soup
   1 can cream of celery soup

1 stick margarine
1 1/2 cups cooked rice
3/4 cup water or sherry
4 or 5 boneless chicken breasts, cut in half

Blend soups, margarine, and water (or sherry) together over low heat. Mix half of soup mixture with 1 1/2 cups uncooked rice (not instant rice) and pour into 9 x 13-inch baking dish. Place chicken breasts on top of rice, then pour remaining soup mixture over chicken. Sprinkle with paprika and cover with foil. Bake at 275° for 3 hours.

Complete the meal with a green vegetable or potatoes au gratin.

● ● ● ● ● ● ● ●

Related Scripture

Remember not the sins of my youth and my rebellious ways; according to your love remember me, for you are good, O LORD.

Psalm 25:7

High school is often a time of testing and challenging. Although we often remember the good times, we tend to forget the struggles and pain: conflicts with parents, the ups and downs of romance, the pressures to conform to questionable behavior, and so on. Happily, God is able to help us through those times and to forgive us when we make selfish choices.

Discussion Questions

Icebreakers

1. Who was your favorite teacher in high school?
2. What was your most embarrassing moment in front of your classmates?
3. What crowd did you run around with in high school? How would your classmates have characterized you?

4. What cross-town or cross-county adversary was your school's most intense rival?
5. What was your worst date in high school?
6. What were your grades like in a typical semester?

Getting Serious

7. What is the most difficult challenge you had to face in school?
8. Would you want to relive your high school experience again? Why or why not?
9. Where did you think your life was headed after graduation? Has it turned out as you expected, or did it take some surprising turns?
10. What did you learn in high school (not necessarily book knowledge) that you've carried with you through life?
11. What words of advice would you give to a high-schooler today?
12. How can you see God's guidance in your life during the high school years, perhaps in ways that at the time you could not understand?

Wrap-up

If your guests attended different schools, have each guest sing his or her high school fight song or favorite cheer. Give a prize to the person who sings with the most enthusiasm and conviction. If everyone went to the same school, sing your fight song or raise the cheer together.

Another possibility is to have your guests write an essay of one hundred words called "What I Did During My Last Summer Vacation." Encourage them to read their compositions aloud.

Lifestyles of the Rich and Famous Evening

Theme

Invite your guests to enjoy a night in high society. For a few hours, they'll be the idols of millions and the talk of the town.

Dress

Encourage your guests to wear their ritziest and glitziest. Men might wear an old tuxedo or their best suit. Women should dig out any formal wear from proms or weddings (taffeta preferred). Accessorize with rhinestones, rings, glitzy costume jewelry, and faux pearls.

Decorations

This is a night for your finest. Dig out white tablecloths and your best china. Dine by candlelight with music playing softly in the background. Enlist some youth from the church to play your butler and maid. Have other youth play the paparazzi (photographers who photograph celebrities). When your guests arrive, have your "butler" announce them. Have the paparazzi clamor and snap their pictures.

Music

Play only classical music this evening—keep the volume low. Baroque and classical period composers would be tasteful choices: try J. S. Bach, Handel, Haydn, Mozart, and Vivaldi.

Mixers and Games

Celebrity Auction

Give each guest $100,000 in play money. (You may make the play money yourself or use currency provided in such games as Monopoly or Life.) If you don't want to use play money, give each person a credit line of $100,000. Appoint a guest to serve as accountant to make sure that guests don't overspend their limit.

Then present a number of "celebrity" items for auction. You can actually display objects or ask your guests to imagine them. Guests should bid according to their personal tastes and appreciation for the celebrity. The bidding for all items starts at $10,000. You may want to announce the list before the auction starts.

A letter signed by Abraham Lincoln
A dress worn by Vivien Leigh in *Gone with the Wind*
A rare $20 gold piece
Inaugural gown worn by Jackie Kennedy
A newly discovered Gutenberg Bible
A mechanical dinosaur from *Jurassic Park*
Babe Ruth's uniform
Shirt worn by Elvis Presley in *Blue Hawaii*
Manuscript of *Hamlet* autographed by William Shakespeare
Claude Monet's Impressionist painting "Water Lilies"
Guitar played by Beatle Paul McCartney on Ed Sullivan show
First-century manuscript of the Gospel of Mark
Trench coat worn by Peter Falk on *Columbo*
Billy Graham's boyhood home
Bowl of jellybeans from Ronald Reagan's White House desk

Shoes worn by Michael Jordan in NBA finals
Archie Bunker's chair
Autographed score of Handel's *Messiah*
Piano owned by Harry S. Truman
The cape worn by Michael Keaton in *Batman*
Wardrobe owned by C. S. Lewis

A B C Celebrity

This rapid-fire game requires quick responses. Starting with the letter *A*, select a person to name a movie or television star (living or dead) whose last name begins with that letter (examples: Fred Astaire, Alan Alda, Tim Allen). That person then selects another guest to name a celebrity whose last name begins with *B*. He or she has five seconds to respond; if time expires, that person is out, and a new person is selected. Everyone in the group must have had the opportunity to reply before a guest can be chosen again. Continue in this manner until the alphabet is completed or until one person remains.

You may want to throw out the letters *Q*, *X*, and *Z* to keep the game going. If you want to make the game more challenging, have guests name stars whose first and last names begin with the same letter.

Who Said It?

Have your guests match the celebrity with these well-known quotes.

1. "Hold on there, pilgrim."   a. Greta Garbo
2. "Zuzu's petals!"   b. Bob Hope
3. "When I'm good, I'm good.   c. Groucho Marx
   When I'm bad, I'm better."
4. "I vant to be alone."   d. Will Rogers
5. "Thanks for the memories."   e. Jimmy Stewart
6. "Go away, kid, you bother me."   f. Sally Field
7. "I never met a man I didn't like."   g. Bette Davis

(continued)

8. "Buckle your seat belt, it's going   h. Steve Martin
   to be a bumpy night."
9. "Hello, I must be going."   i. George Bush
10. "You like me. You really like me."   j. Vivien Leigh
11. "Well, excuuuuuuuse me!"   k. John Wayne
12. "Go ahead, make my day."   l. Mae West
13. "Read my lips."   m. Clint Eastwood
14. "Tomorrow is another day."   n. W. C. Fields

Answers: 1. k; 2. e; 3. l; 4. a; 5. b; 6. n; 7. d; 8. g; 9. c; 10. f; 11. h; 12. m; 13. i; 14. j

● ● ● ● ● ● ● ●

Menu

Appetizers: Chicken Log
Ingredients
2 8-ounce packages cream cheese
2 cans chunky chicken
1/2 teaspoon curry powder
1 tablespoon Worcestershire sauce
1/3 cup chopped celery
1/4 cup snipped parsley
slivered almonds

Mix cheese, Worcestershire sauce, and curry powder. Mix in other ingredients. Refrigerate 3 to 4 hours. Roll in slivered almonds. Serve on crackers or cucumber rounds.

Serve your appetizers on silver trays. Line your trays with paper doilies.

Main Dish: Barbecued Flank Steak. This recipe is great for entertaining because everything is done ahead of time.
Ingredients
3 to 4 pounds flank steak

Liquid Smoke
celery salt
garlic salt
onion salt
1 teaspoon Worcestershire sauce
1 cup barbecue sauce

Place the steaks in a baking dish so they lie relatively flat. Sprinkle the steaks with Liquid Smoke, celery, garlic, and onion salt. Cover with aluminum foil and refrigerate overnight. Six hours before serving, add salt and pepper (if desired) and Worcestershire sauce. Bake at 275° for 4 hours. Drain off the liquid and add barbecue sauce. Bake 1 more hour. Serve with additional barbecue sauce.

Alternate Main Dish: Red Glazed Pork Chops (see recipe in the 1950s supper club evening).

Dessert: Texas Millionaire Pie
Ingredients
1 20-ounce can crushed pineapple
1 14-ounce can Eagle Brand milk
1 cup chopped pecans
3 tablespoons lemon juice concentrate
1 9-ounce carton whipped topping
1 9-inch graham cracker pie shell

Mix all ingredients; fold in whipped topping. Pour into pie shell and refrigerate until serving time.

Related Scripture

But godliness with contentment is great gain. For we brought nothing into the world, and we can take nothing out of it. But if we have food and clothing, we will be content with that. People who want to get rich fall into temptation and a trap and into many foolish and harmful desires that plunge men into ruin and destruction. For the love of money is a root of all kinds of evil.

Some people, eager for money, have wandered from the faith and pierced themselves with many griefs.

1 Timothy 6:6–10

This Scripture speaks of being content with what we have. It stresses the point that we bring nothing into the world and that we take nothing out of it. This Scripture is a very clear command from God regarding how we are to view being "rich and famous." You may want to read this after you cover the discussion questions.

Discussion Questions

Icebreakers

1. Who is your favorite celebrity and why?
2. What celebrity do you like the least? Why?
3. What luxury gives you twinges of guilt?
4. What amount of money would make you feel rich?
5. If you were rich, how would your current lifestyle change?
6. What luxury in your life could you absolutely not do without?

Getting Serious

7. Why are many people tight-lipped about their financial status?
8. What luxuries would be hardest for you to give up?
9. Should Christians be rich?
10. Is there a point where wealth would be detrimental to a Christian's witness?
11. Is there anything wrong with a Christian playing the lottery?
12. Why did Jesus say that it's easier for a camel to go through the eye of a needle than for a rich man to enter the kingdom of heaven?

Wrap-up

Ask your guests to imagine that they had $1 million to spend on anyone but themselves. Have each person discuss how he or she would spend that money.

SPORTS EVENING

Theme

Your house will be rockin' as guests assemble to compete in games and test their sports knowledge. As your guests enter the front door, announce their names in a loud, melodramatic voice, as if you were giving the starting lineups at a basketball game. Play crowd noises in the background.

Dress

Guests may wear clothing featuring the names and logos of their favorite teams. Hats, sweatshirts, sweatpants, jerseys, T-shirts, and athletic shoes are ideal. More adventurous people may want to bring along equipment such as bats, gloves, hockey sticks, football helmets, and soccer balls. Regardless of what they choose, their clothing should be loose-fitting and comfortable. Guests will be participating in light athletic activity.

Decorations

What sports night would be complete without pennants? Add several college and pro team flags to your rooms. Posters of star athletes will add motion and color. If you have a VCR, rent a tape featuring great moments in sports and play it with the sound turned down. Toss around a few Nerf footballs or let guests sink a few free throws with a child's foam ball and basketball goal.

Music

Your public library may have a record or cassette that features the fight songs of college teams. You can play other popular sporting event favorites that will annoy or amuse your guests: "We Will Rock You/We Are the Champions" by Queen; "Rock and Roll (Part 2)" by Gary Glitter; "Na Na Hey Hey (Kiss Him Goodbye)" by Steam; "Theme from Rocky (Gonna Fly Now)" by Bill Conti; and "Eye of the Tiger" by Survivor. If you have an electronic keyboard, maybe a talented guest will volunteer to play ballpark favorites such as "Take Me Out to the Ballgame."

Mixers and Games

Matching Mascots

Challenge your guests to test their knowledge of college sports mascots. Have them write the number of the college in the blank next to the correct nickname. (Answers are on p. 97.)

1. Penn State	_____	Vandals
2. Maryland	_____	Red Raiders
3. Hawaii	_____	Cyclones
4. UCLA	_____	Terrapins
5. Washington State	_____	Gators
6. Wisconsin	_____	Scarlet Knights
7. Arkansas	_____	Razorbacks
8. Idaho	_____	Wolfpack
9. Boston College	_____	Wildcats
10. Vanderbilt	_____	Nittany Lions
11. North Carolina State	_____	Bruins
12. Florida	_____	Commodores
13. Iowa State	_____	Rainbows

14. Temple   _____ Owls
15. Texas Tech   _____ Badgers
16. Louisville   _____ Orangemen
17. Northwestern   _____ Cardinals
18. Oregon   _____ Cougars
19. Syracuse   _____ Golden Eagles
20. Rutgers   _____ Ducks

Answers to Matching Mascots: Vandals—8; Red Raiders—15; Cyclones—13; Terrapins—2; Gators—12; Scarlet Knights—20; Razorbacks—7; Wolfpack—11; Wildcats—17; Nittany Lions—1; Bruins—4; Commodores—10; Rainbows—3, Owls—14; Badgers—6; Orangemen—19; Cardinals—16; Cougars—5; Golden Eagles—9; Ducks—18.

24-Second Shot Clock

Divide the group into two teams. Give the first team a stopwatch (or a watch with a second hand) and a pencil and notepad. The second team is to draw a letter of the alphabet out of a hat (you should prepare this beforehand). Using an appointed spokesperson, the second team is to name all the professional athletes (past and present) they can think of whose last names begin with that letter. The other team is to record their answers and cut them off after 24 seconds. Tally the score, and then give the other team a chance to draw a letter and name names. Continue for three or four rounds. High score wins.

Legends of the Game

Give each guest a slip of paper and a pencil. Then have everyone complete the sentence, "My greatest athletic achievement was _____." When they are finished, have them fold the slips of paper and hand them to you or a designated guest. Read each one aloud, and have the group try to decide who achieved each feat. Other statements you might try include: "My greatest thrill as a sports spectator was _____." Or "The sport I can't stand to watch is _____." Have guests elaborate on their answers.

Indoor/Outdoor Olympiad

You might want to generate a little friendly competition—either indoors or outdoors, depending on the weather and the size of your house. Guests should be placed on evenly divided teams. Indoor events could include billiards, Ping-Pong, a beanbag toss, or a Nerf basketball shoot-out. For outdoor events, try a free throw contest, a Frisbee-throwing accuracy test, a volleyball or badminton match, or croquet. Add handicaps (for example, right-handed people can use only their left hands, people shooting the basketball must wear a blindfold) to make the competition more interesting.

● ● ● ● ● ● ● ● ●

Menu

Appetizers: What else? Peanuts, popcorn, and potato chips

Main Dish: Pizza Casserole
Ingredients
 2 pounds ground beef
 1 large onion, chopped
 1-pound box of sea shell macaroni
 1 32-ounce jar of Ragu spaghetti sauce
 1 package of sliced pepperoni
 1 16-ounce package of shredded pizza cheese

Brown ground beef and onion. Drain. Cook and drain sea shells. Mix together with spaghetti sauce. Add pepperoni slices and top with cheese. Bake at 350° for 30 to 45 minutes. (Serves 12.)

Alternate Main Dish: Sloppy joes, fried chicken, or pizza

Dessert: Chocolate cake

● ● ● ● ● ● ● ● ●

Related Scripture

> Do you not know that in a race all the runners run, but only one gets the prize? Run in such a way as to get the prize.
>
> 1 Corinthians 9:24

Athletic events were common even in Paul's day. Then, as now, contestants had to train to achieve mastery of their events. Paul realized that spiritual excellence could not be obtained without dedication. He encouraged Christians to engage in sacrificial, rigorous training to obtain the prize—the eternal inheritance of God's kingdom.

Discussion Questions

Icebreakers

1. What is the most memorable sporting event you've ever attended?
2. What sports teams did your parents root for?
3. What sport do you enjoy playing the most?
4. How do you react when your favorite team loses?
5. How do you feel when you hear a pro athlete complain that he or she isn't getting enough money?
6. What is the worst injury you ever received while participating in a sporting event?

Getting Serious

7. Why do you think Americans have become so crazy about sports?
8. What harmful effects do you see coming from the emphasis on sports and athletes?
9. Why are Americans in general such out-of-shape couch potatoes despite their love for sporting events?
10. What are the benefits and drawbacks of competition?
11. Why does the apostle Paul liken the Christian life to a race?
12. How would you describe your spiritual training regimen?

Wrap-up

Post-Game Show

Have one guest volunteer to be a sports reporter. Have him or her interview the other guests about their particular accomplishments or about the highlights of the evening. Use a video camera to tape this event. Have guests duplicate the form they used for scoring a winning shot or point. Encourage them to use as many sports clichés as possible as they respond to the questions. Stock phrases such as "We were pumped up for these guys," "We never quit," "We gave 110 percent," "We justed wanted it more than they did," "It ain't over until the fat lady sings," and, of course, "I'm going to Disneyland!" would be appropriate. Play back the videotape for guests.

TACKy EVeNiNG

Theme

Have you ever wanted to throw manners and social convention out the window? Here's your chance to laugh with your guests during an evening of low-class, tacky fun. New acquaintances won't have to worry about what they're wearing or whether they're saying the right things. For a truly tacky touch, send out invitations using old invitations. Simply cross out the old information and write in the new. Tonight, anything goes!

Dress

Invite your guests to wear tacky clothes. Award a prize for the best outfit. If your guests aren't the adventuresome types, provide some tacky accessories for them. Visit a local thrift store and purchase ties, scarves, jewelry, and hats. As your guests arrive, give them the accessories to put on. Just a touch of tacky can ruin even the most stylish combination.

Decorations

For this evening, the key words are *plastic* and *clash*. Anything that is the least bit elegant and sophisticated is out. Use the ideas in the recipes section to set your table. Dig out all those garage sale items to use as prizes and party favors. Any black velvet paintings you can get your hands on will be cherished by your guests. Wear your loudest synthetic clothes. As a host you will need to set the tone. Your goal is to get your guests to relax and forget about style and society's rules.

Music

Bad instrumental arrangements of popular songs are a must! You can find collections of these horrors on cassettes in many discount stores. Another surefire crowd pleaser will be disco-tized versions of classical tunes, often complete with drumbeat and chorus. Again, many record stores carry such items. Finally, don't forget old albums by those forgettable recording artists of the 1960s and 1970s—your basic instincts should tell you how to identify the tackiest of the bunch.

Mixers and Games

Tacky Tribulations

Read the following statements one at a time to your guests. Have a couple of people (or if time permits, all of your guests) volunteer to complete each statement with a memorable story.

> The tackiest wedding ceremony I've ever attended was . . .
> The tackiest hotel/motel I've ever stayed at was . . .
> The tackiest outfit I wore to high school was . . .
> The tackiest sitcom I've seen in the past five years was . . .
> The tackiest thing anyone has ever said to me was . . .
> The tackiest bumper sticker I've ever seen said . . .
> The tackiest sermon I can remember hearing was . . .
> The tackiest country-and-western song I can remember was . . .
> The tackiest appetizer I've ever been served at a party was . . .
> The tackiest Christmas lawn display I can remember was . . .

Tacky Tidings

Purchase an assortment of greeting cards (many can be purchased for considerable discounts after holidays). Give each guest a card. Their task is to cross out and/or add new messages to "recycle" the card for a different greeting. For example, a sympathy card might become a birthday card. Have the guests share their creations with the group.

Woeful Walls

Divide the group into smaller groups. Give each group a large sheet of paper and markers. Ask your guests to create the tackiest wallpaper print possible. Give a prize for the tackiest paper.

• • • • • • • •

Menu

Main Dish: Fast food or frozen dinners. Be sure to leave the wrappers and containers around for your guests to see. Serve your food on paper plates or mismatched dishes. Use all those cups from sporting events, fast food restaurants, and gas station promotions. Use napkins left over from previous celebrations.

Dessert: Dirt Pudding
Ingredients
   1 package Oreo cookies, crumbled
   1 8-ounce package cream cheese
   1 cup powdered sugar
   1/2 stick margarine
   2 small boxes French vanilla instant pudding
   3 1/2 cups milk
   1 8-ounce carton whipped topping

Mix together cream cheese, powdered sugar, and margarine. In a separate bowl, mix pudding with milk. Add to cream cheese mixture. Fold in whipped topping.

Using a large terra-cotta planter, layer cookies and pudding until full. Stick in some plastic flowers and serve to your guests as if it were the ultimate in gourmet desserts.

● ● ● ● ● ● ● ●

Related Scripture

Do not love the world or anything in the world. If anyone loves the world, the love of the Father is not in him.

1 John 2:15

They loved praise from men more than praise from God.

John 12:43

These verses warn us not to seek the approval of the world, but of God. As Christians, we are called to be different. We are called to be lights in a world of darkness. This is difficult because the world's approval is tangible, while God's can seem quite remote. How can we help each other to be different, living examples of God's love?

Discussion Questions

Icebreakers

1. Of all the clothing looks of recent times, which one is your favorite? Why?
2. What are your least favorite clothing styles?
3. What is one fad or style that you have gone along with but secretly hated?
4. What tacky possessions of yours are lurking in a basement or attic?
5. How realistically is our society portrayed on TV?
6. How do you react when given a well-intended but tacky gift?

Getting Serious

7. Who or what determines what is in and out in our society?

8. When have you "dared to be different," even though it cost you popularity or friends?
9. To what extent should a Christian follow the norm? Apply this question to the following categories: (a) dress (b) entertainment (c) work (d) speech (e) possessions.
10. How does our society treat people who are different from the norm?
11. In what areas do you still struggle with conformity to the world's expectations?
12. In what ways are Christians called to be different?

Wrap-up

Before the meeting, tell your guests to visit one of those stores where everything is a dollar or less. Have them purchase the tackiest object they can find. When your guests arrive, have them put the objects (still in bags) in another room. As discussion time winds down, have your guests retrieve their purchases and share their finds.

STAR TREK EVENING

Theme

Beam your guests up for a night aboard the Starship *Enterprise*. You'll go where no men have gone before during this evening of futuristic fun.

Dress

For an all-out Trekkie adventure, have your guests dress as their favorite *Star Trek* characters. If your guests are a bit hesitant, have them dress in long-sleeved shirts and dark pants. As they arrive, you can stick an *Enterprise* emblem on their shirts.

Decorations

Cover your walls with white butcher paper. On the paper, draw a large TV screen, various buttons, and complex electronic setups. Use walkie-talkies to talk to your spouse or other guests. For a creative touch, use a video camera to tape a message from a "space alien" for you and your guests. The alien could welcome the guests, explain the purpose of the evening, and perhaps warn of an evil plot afoot. Play the tape for your guests to start the evening.

Music

If you can't locate music from the various *Star Trek* series, play ethe-real electronic music to create a proper "spaced out" mood. Such music is available from larger record stores or libraries.

Mixers and Games

Bands of Truth

From construction paper, cut strips long enough to fit around an adult's head. On the strips, write the questions listed below. When your guests arrive, have them close their eyes while you fasten the headbands around their heads. The headbands should be positioned so that the questions can be read by others. Each guest is to ask the other guests to answer his or her question. The task is to figure out the question based on the answers received.

1. How will you spend your retirement?
2. What current technology could you not live without?
3. Who is your favorite *Star Trek* character?
4. What is your favorite *Star Trek* episode?
5. How many of the *Star Trek* movies have you seen?
6. What part of growing old do you hate the most?
7. What planet would you like to visit?
8. What is your favorite science fiction movie?
9. What were you doing when the astronauts first walked on the moon?
10. What person in this room has the logical powers of Dr. Spock?

Captain's Log

This mixer is similar to the popular party game Mad Libs. Before you begin reading the story, go through and fill in each blank by ask-ing your guests to provide the kind of word listed in parentheses. Do not give away any of the story as you do this. After all of the blanks have been completed, read the story aloud.

Starship *Enterprise,* ship's log, stardate _____(a date). Due to an emergency 911 call, Captain James T. Kirk had taken a leave of absence from his command. Fleet commanders had placed Major _____(a guest) in temporary command. The *Enterprise* had been running along very smoothly when crew member _____(another guest) noticed a strange noise. It sounded like _____(a strange noise). The crew member notified the Major immediately. The Major, knowing that immediate action was required, called, "Spock, get me_____ (a third guest) at once. This job calls for our best _____ (an occupation)."

"I am sorry, Major," replied Mr. Spock. "He is currently with Bones undergoing a _____(a common operation)."

"Well then," exclaimed the Major, "get me the second best. Get me _____(a fourth guest)."

"Unfortunately," informed Mr. Spock, "he is in the _____ (vacation spot) honeymooning."

"_____(an exclamation)!" shouted the Major. "Who is available?" At that very moment all of the *Enterprise's* equipment shut down. The interspace TV phone lit up. A strange alien came on the screen. "Why, he looks just like _____(a famous person)," observed one of the crew members.

"I am _____(a fifth guest) from _____ (a fictional planet). We have sabotaged your ship. In ten minutes we will board and remove all of your _____(a performer) albums. We promise no one will be hurt." The screen went blank and the equipment came back on.

"I think it would be in our best interest to surrender the albums peacefully," advised Mr. Spock.

"Are you crazy?" shouted the Major. "Do you have any idea what the market value of those albums is?"

"I believe _____(a dollar amount) per album is the fair market value. You can get them for _____(a dollar amount) if you order through _____(a mail order firm)," answered Mr. Spock.

"And you want to surrender them peacefully," grumbled the Major. "Besides, they remind me of _____(an event). No, they are much too valuable. We must fix the *Enterprise* at once. Is there no one else who could help us?"

"We could call _____(a local repair shop)," suggested Scottie.

"Excellent idea!" bellowed the Major. The call was made but unfortunately the repair shop had a waiting list. They could not make a service call for _____(a number) days.

In a last desperate measure, the Major called his _____(a female relative). She told him to take a _____(an item found in a woman's purse) and put it in the computer and turn four times. Then the crew should sing _____ (a song).

With only two minutes left, Scottie followed the instructions. Suddenly the noise stopped. The crew cheered as the *Enterprise* sped away.

"Well done, Major," said Mr. Spock. The Major simply nodded. He was looking ahead to retirement. He planned to retire to _____(a place) and spend his days listening to the albums while he _____(a leisure activity). The ship's log was closed.

● ● ● ● ● ● ● ●
Menu

Beverage: Tang. After all, it is the drink of astronauts.

Main Dish: Bones's Spare Ribs
Ingredients
 3–4 pounds spare ribs
 1 6-ounce bottle of soy sauce
 1 can consommé
 1 lemon (juice only)
 1/4 teaspoon garlic salt
 paprika

Sauce
1 cup catsup
4 tablespoons vinegar
4 tablespoons brown sugar
4 tablespoons Worcestershire sauce
2 teaspoons Liquid Smoke

Soak ribs overnight in soy sauce, consommé, lemon juice, and garlic salt. Sprinkle with paprika. Make the sauce by mixing all the ingredients except Liquid Smoke; simmer 10 minutes and then add Liquid Smoke. Drain liquid from meat and cover meat with sauce. Bake at 350° until meat is tender.

Serve with a salad and baked potatoes.

Dessert: Angel food cake. Have fruit sauce, chocolate sauce, and whipped cream on hand for toppings.

● ● ● ● ● ● ● ●

Related Scripture

Therefore do not worry about tomorrow, for tomorrow will worry about itself. Each day has enough trouble of its own.

Matthew 6:34

Why, you do not even know what will happen tomorrow. What is your life? You are a mist that appears for a little while and then vanishes.

James 4:14

Both of these verses admonish us not to worry about tomorrow, but to concern ourselves with the day at hand. Concern for our world, our children, and our environment is all a part of good stewardship. When we become consumed by the future, however, we often become self-centered. There is much to do today. God has taken care of our future so that we can do his work today.

Discussion Questions

Icebreakers

1. What gadgets or technology on *Star Trek* fascinate you?
2. What technological innovations of the last ten years have intrigued you the most?
3. What character in the *Star Trek* series or movies do you identify with most strongly?
4. What aspects of the future portrayed in *Star Trek* disturb you?
5. Why do you think *Star Trek* remains popular to this day?
6. What books or movies about the future have made a strong impression on you?

Getting Serious

7. Do you believe that there is life in other parts of the universe? Why or why not?
8. What aspect about our society's future do you find frightening?
9. What aspect about your family's future do you find frightening?
10. If you could be shown any one part of your future, what would you want to see?
11. What do you think will happen to our planet in the next one hundred years?
12. What should we do to prepare for the future?

Wrap-up

Rent an episode of the *Star Trek* television series and view it with your guests. Afterward, discuss the important themes and funny observations.

TV TRIVIA EVENING

Theme

Tonight your guests will tune in and zone out at an evening dedicated to TV land. Your guests need only bring their vast knowledge of TV lore. For once, being a couch potato is in!

Dress

It goes without saying that your guests should come as favorite TV characters. Award a prize for the most imaginative costume.

Decorations

Borrow a few portable sets from neighbors and friends, and have all the sets playing when your guests arrive. Have posters or pictures from old and new television shows scattered around the room.

Music

Many television theme songs have crossed over to score big on the pop charts. Several shows have had their own soundtracks. You should be able to find collections of TV theme songs on cassettes or CDs at modest prices.

Mixers and Games

Telepardy

This game, based on TV trivia, is a version of the popular show *Jeopardy*. Because it is rather long and involved, you may want to play this after you eat.

On poster boards, write the categories (listed below) at the top. Underneath, write the point values: 1000, 800, 600, 400, and 200. Divide the group into two teams. Flip a coin to determine who goes first. The winning team picks a category and a point value. Upon hearing the clue, they have thirty seconds to provide an answer, which must be phrased as a question. If their answer is correct, they are awarded the points assigned for that question, and the team selects another question. If the team is unable to answer the question, however, the other team gets a chance to answer the same question for double the point value. Keep a running total of the score. Give the winning team copies of *TV Guide*.

TV Occupations: Give the occupation of these characters.

1000 Steven Keaton of *Family Ties* (Who is a program director for a PBS station?)

800 Mary Richards of *The Mary Tyler Moore Show* (Who is a television producer?)

600 Howard Cunningham of *Happy Days* (Who is a hardware store owner?)

400 Mike Brady of *The Brady Bunch* (Who is an architect?)

200 Fred Flintstone of *The Flintstones* (Who is a quarry worker?)

TV Children: Name the children in these TV families.

1000 The Waltons (Who are John-Boy, Mary Ellen, Jason, Ben, Erin, Jim-Bob, and Elizabeth?)

800 The Brady Bunch (Who are Greg, Peter, Bobby, Marcia, Jan, and Cindy?)

600 The Huxtables of *The Cosby Show* (Who are Sondra, Denise, Theo, Vanessa, and Rudy?)

400 The Conners of *Roseanne* (Who are Becky, Darlene, and D. J.?)

200 The Douglases of *My Three Sons* (Who are Rob, Chip, and Ernie? [Mike may also be mentioned.])

TV Detectives: Provide the *character* names of these TV detectives.

1000 With Dan-o's help, he kept crime off the islands. (Who is Steve McGarrett?)

800 This P.I.'s favorite team was the Detroit Tigers. (Who is Magnum?)

600 This former hillbilly cleaned up his act to investigate crime. (Who is Barnaby Jones?)

400 He owns a 1960 Peugeot and a collection of bad cigars. (Who is Columbo?)

200 She takes murder quite literally. (Who is Jessica Fletcher?)

TV Best Friends: Name these characters' friends and sidekicks.

1000 Dobie Gillis (Who is Maynard Krebs?)

800 Michael Stedman of *thirtysomething* (Who is Elliot Weston?)

600 Mary Richards (Who is Rhoda Morgenstern?)

400 Lucy Ricardo (Who is Ethel Mertz?)

200 Kevin Arnold (Who is Paul Pfeiffer?)

TV Multiple Personalities: Given the following actor or actress and one of the shows in which he or she starred, name another show in which he or she also played a central character.

1000 Robert Conrad, *The Wild Wild West* (What is *Black Sheep Squadron?*)

800 Don Knotts, *The Andy Griffith Show* (What is *Three's Company?*)

600 Susan Dey, *L.A. Law* (What is *The Partridge Family* or *Love and War?*)

400 Jane Curtin, *Saturday Night Live* (What is *Kate & Allie?*)

200 Harry Morgan, *M*A*S*H* (What is *Dragnet?*)

Stump the Band

Divide into two groups. One side is to announce the theme song to a television show and then sing the first line of that song. The other side has to come up with the next line. If it can, the turn goes back to the first team, which then has to come up with the third line. If it cannot, the first side receives two points. Continue until the song is completed or until a team fails to come up with a line. Appoint a knowledgeable TV buff to judge questionable song lines!

Network Difficulties

Again, this game will work best between two evenly divided teams. Write the names of the following shows on slips of paper or small cards. (Provide two sets, one for each team.) The teams are to group the shows according to the major networks on which they first appeared. Tell the teams that each network will have eight shows. When both teams are finished, check the results and announce the number of correct answers for each network. Give the teams a chance to make corrections and then recheck their answers. The team with the highest number of correct answers wins.

CBS
Gilligan's Island
Hawaii Five-O
Dallas
Gunsmoke
The Carol Burnett Show
Northern Exposure
The Beverly Hillbillies
All in the Family

NBC
L.A. Law
Family Ties
Little House on the Prairie
Hill Street Blues
The Golden Girls
St. Elsewhere
The Rockford Files
Get Smart

ABC
Happy Days
The Brady Bunch
Charlie's Angels

The Wonder Years
20/20
The Love Boat
Marcus Welby M.D.
The Odd Couple

● ● ● ● ● ● ● ●

Menu

Appetizers: egg rolls, microwave fries, or popcorn. Be sure to leave food items in their trays so that your guests make the TV connection.

Main Dish: Marion Cunningham's Party Meat Loaf
Ingredients
2 pounds ground beef
1 cup bread crumbs
1 egg
2 small cans tomato sauce
1 teaspoon onion salt
1 teaspoon garlic salt
2 teaspoons oregano
mozzarella cheese, sliced

Mix all the ingredients, except one can of tomato sauce and the cheese. Flatten out on a larger sheet of wax paper until you have a large rectangle. Place cheese on top. Roll up jelly-roll style and seal ends. Place in pan and bake at 350° for 1 hour. Drain off liquid and pour second small can of tomato sauce over the top. Bake 15 more minutes.

Dessert: Brady Bunch Brownies
Ingredients
3/4 cup melted margarine
1 1/2 cups sugar
1 1/2 teaspoons vanilla

3 eggs
3/4 cup flour
1/2 cup cocoa
1/2 teaspoon baking powder
1/2 teaspoon salt
1 cup semi-sweet chocolate chips

Heat oven to 350°. Grease 8" x 8" x 2" pan. Blend melted margarine, sugar, and vanilla. Add eggs, beat well with spoon. Combine flour, cocoa, baking powder, and salt and gradually add to egg mixture, beating well until blended. Stir in chips. Spread in prepared pan. Bake 40 to 45 minutes or until brownies begin to pull away from sides of pan. Cool completely. Sprinkle with powdered sugar. Serves eight.

• • • • • • • •

Related Scripture

Therefore, I urge you, brothers, in view of God's mercy, to offer your bodies as living sacrifices, holy and pleasing to God—this is your spiritual act of worship. Do not conform any longer to the pattern of this world, but be transformed by the renewing of your mind. Then you will be able to test and approve what God's will is—his good, pleasing and perfect will.

Romans 12:1–2

This Scripture passage instructs us to keep our bodies (and thoughts) acceptable to God, to keep them free of the world's influence. This text stands in contrast to the questionable and outright harmful ideas pushed at us by television. We must respect the power of this medium and avoid contact with its secular values as we seek to lead godly lives.

Discussion Questions

Icebreakers

1. What was your favorite show as a child?

2. What TV shows did your parents dislike?
3. What is the most memorable event you ever saw on television?
4. What shows are your favorites now?
5. What do you feel is the biggest change TV has made in our society over the years?
6. What are the positive trends in TV today?

Getting Serious

7. What are the most serious problems that television creates for our society?
8. Some critics think the appropriate response to TV is for people to stop watching it altogether. Do you think this suggestion is practical? Why or why not?
9. When was the last time you switched channels because of the objectionable content of a program?
10. What TV commercials do you find annoying or offensive?
11. In what ways does TV hinder communication between family members? Do you think this is a serious problem?
12. Suppose Christ first came to the earth in the 1990s. How would TV have impacted his ministry? Would he have used TV?

Wrap-up

Watch an episode of a TV show from the 1950s or 1960s (many are available on videocassette). Have guests think of all the ways that television has changed since then.